MW00944652

MY NAME IS JACKSON

Prison Without Walls

by

J. L. Erwin

Copyright 2023 by J. L. Erwin

Dedication

If you are one of those people, Policemen in particular, who are doing the right things, those things may appear unnoticed by the many, but I can assure you your acts of kindness will not be forgotten by those you have helped.

I want to dedicate this work to the people who did what was right, although, because of the views of the particular area of the country where I grew up, it would probably have been viewed differently if discovered at the time. For me, this was the cop who would look for a kid to drive him home (in the front seat of the cop car), would notice if he hadn't eaten, and, pretending to be hungry, would buy the kid a hamburger, French fries, and a coke. Aside from myself, I know there must have been others. He was truly one of the good ones.

Although he later became the chief of police, I never stopped calling him Lieutenant. I met him while I was in grade school. By continually looking out for me, he showed me that cops weren't the bad guys. Because of him, I would like to dedicate this work to every cop who does what is right in bad situations but has never been acknowledged for it. To my knowledge, my lieutenant was never seen for the good man that he was, but I can assure you he changed the course of my life for the better. He may have actually been my very first Hero.

One of life's ironies is that we tend to suppress the memory of the good things because of so many bad things. The good memories only resurface after our hero has passed. My cop knew I learned to trust him. He changed the way I looked at people in authority. But as happens so often, by the time I finally began to realize his impact on me fully, he had already passed.

Contents

Foreword

As a licensed Marriage and Family Therapist for years, I have learned and seen firsthand what an abusive childhood and generational trauma can do to people. Meeting Joe in our Veterans Writers group showed me what it looks like to be a survivor.

Throughout the years, I have gotten pieces of his upbringing and realized how resilient Joe is despite his background. This book has helped me understand that some people are just special; Joe is one of them. His willingness to be open about the horrors of his childhood is something very few are willing to do outside of a therapy room. Joe is fearless in discussing the severity of his abuse. Joe is a unicorn. His ability to grow, become successful, and make positive choices makes him the perfect person to look up to for those who have been abused.

Friends, family, police, therapists, doctors, and pastors say they understand, but do they? To truly understand you must walk through the life of an abused child to truly understand how the abuse can define someone. Most people can empathize; it takes living the abuse in your life to understand truly.

Abuse comes in two forms: physical and verbal. Joe has survived both, but verbal abuse can be worse. Bruises and broken bones can heal, and words can stay forever. In an abusive household, the abused has a skewed idea of normal. Everyone has a different version of normal. The abuse is especially horrific when the abusers are the ones who are supposed to protect you. As a child, this isn't very clear and can cause you to question everything you do and say for your entire life. Family lines are crossed, and boundaries are run over with little to no recourse. In an abusive household, silence is expected. Discussing the truth is forbidden and has significant consequences inside and outside the house. Challenging the abuser takes on another level of fear. Staying silent even when you know better becomes your routine. The horrors of Joe's childhood cause him to blame himself for not speaking up or standing up to the abusers. This is common and can become a lifelong struggle for self-forgiveness. Society lends a blind eye to awfulness in most cases regarding abused children, especially in the South and the timeframe of Joe's upbringing. Those who are abused are often groomed to lie, cheat, and steal to maintain family secrets. Joe's experiences of abuse can last a lifetime.

Joe's stories show how robust and resilient our brains and minds can be. Memories have holes because you are being protected from the severity of the abuse. Joe's hole, in his accounts, shows how his brain protects him from what he cannot understand or emotionally handle as he works through the trauma. This book shows the journey Joe is on to make his life better. This is a lifelong journey, and this book is a part of his healing. It shows how he feels and struggles to break the generational trauma imposed on him by his family, society, and the system. If you have lived through an abusive childhood or know someone who has, this book is for you. His willingness to help others who were abused and professionals who work with the victims through his writing is commendable. Joe's courage, vulnerability, and desire to survive should encourage others who have been abused in childhood.

Joe refuses to be a victim; he is a survivor.

Fred "Bo" Dunning M.A, LMFT, USAF Ret.

Author of:

Living the Dream, I & amp; II

Married to PTSD, Stories from the Trenches

Married to PTSD, More Stories from the Trenches

51 Stupid Questions People Ask Veterans.

7 Keys to a Successful PTSD Relationship

Introduction

As I write this introduction, I need to explain the purpose of my writing. They are twofold:

Writing relieves me. I started writing again after my once-removed cousin's arrest for the sex crimes he committed against his adopted children. Another cousin of my uncle and aunt who raised me called to inform me of his arrest. She also called my oldest sister, trying to understand what was happening. I stated amongst the three of us during our three-way call the investigators would want to talk with us during this process. The next evening, my sister informed us that she had contacted the FBI and gave me a number to call to speak with the lead investigator. The investigator asked me to begin writing down my memories of the house. The result is this attempt to explain my lack of a childhood.

That seems simple; it is not a daunting task; it is impossible. I am an abused child, and because of this, I am constantly trying to make sense of the past as I recall it. Therein lies the problem; there is no logical way to explain insanity. While a child, I saw many tragic events, but our minds in some self-protection mode will not release information because it has determined we cannot withstand the pain it would cause.

Thus, my foundation is shaky, and as I write, I am discovering old events as though I am experiencing them for the first time. To make matters worse, I am not discovering them through the man I am today; I discover them through the eyes of the child who witnessed them.

I am continually learning and piecing together my past.

I am not holding back while writing; I am freeing myself. Sometimes, this comes through a painful process, or what I say may strike me as odd. While contemplating these thoughts, I try to release myself and can move on because I was frozen in time when the tragic events happened. The brain trying to protect me has left me with black holes in my memory, which cause me to revisit the tragic events to try to come to grips with the past. Sometimes, I make poor decisions based on misinformation processed instead of the truth of the event. The misinformation my brain has recorded to protect me also hinders me from growing as a person.

Add this to the fact that there are things words will never contain.

There are things that people experience that words cannot communicate. Many know combat to be such an event. Today's soldiers have not experienced the combat that soldiers of the past have endured. The ever-evolving tortures of combat have different effects on the soldiers. Yet combat soldiers can communicate to one another beyond what their words convey. You cannot comprehend the cost of battle through a textbook because the textbook cannot contain the horrors of war.

We abused children have also faced horror, altering how our minds utilize the information. Sometimes, we leave out information because we believe the way we see it is usual, and it would be redundant to give such details. Sometimes, we leave out information because we have been taught that society doesn't want to hear it.

We need to find out society's need for a detailed description. This lack of understanding of what areas society needs to grasp what we're not saying, mingled with the things we continually discover by revisiting our past, makes it impossible to tell my story accurately.

This book is book one of a series. I have begun book two. This book attempts to tell the story of my abuse. The following books will attempt to show the abuse's effects on me. Abuse is a "gift" that keeps unfolding. Accepting the truth alters the foundation upon which I'm left to build my life.

If I do not tell my story, many in society will go through life, never realizing we exist. We victims of abuse are far more common than society cares to admit. It is commonly attributed to Edmund Burke, who said, "The only thing necessary for the triumph of evil is for good men to do nothing." My purpose for this writing is so that the subject becomes addressed by society and for other victims to know that they are not alone. We are not broken. We are different. And it is alright not to desire to be normal when normal is seen as the evil that people do against each other.

I accept the flaws in my account. As my discoveries permit, I will write down my story of the effects of abuse.

J. L. Erwin

MY NAME IS JACKSON

Prison Without Walls

PART ONE

Chapter 1

I've heard the definition of insanity is repeating an action and expecting different results. What is often overlooked are the stumbling blocks we inadvertently set for ourselves. Those soft-spoken inner talks distort our perception of reality. When trapped between such lies, our world is permitted to appear as we believe others have determined it should. We have trapped ourselves in an existence that has us looking into life's mirror, wondering if anyone is there.

This is my account of an abused child. By telling my story, I am discovering ways to free myself. Though, the abuses prevent me from giving a linear history, as others with "normal" lives might. My memories are interwoven with lies. Some lies were taught. Some were lies I used to patch or smooth over the holes of a child's memory who was searching for an explanation. However, the distorting patches dissipate whenever I can face the abuses, and I am left with truths that leave holes in my account. I give my story to allow all to glean the lessons existence has taught so we can move forward and destroy these prisons without walls.

It was not until I was older that I realized the tragedy of a stolen childhood. One's childhood can never be replaced. This is not an account of the abuses; it is the story of the search for life. An understanding of the cost of overcoming. Though many events may appear out of place, I give this account knowing nature seeks balance. The problem being I grew up in an abusive environment. Much as being a leper is expected in a leper colony, an abused person seeking the way of freedom has to fumble along an unknown path. I am not going to give a victim's account. I am not a victim. I am a person who is overcoming being abused.

When a child is trapped in a dangerous situation, whatever they do to exist it is justified. My first cry was one of survival. From there, I was able to choose to live. This yearning was ignited by disturbing glimpses. Which brought opportunities to question the past. The image of what could have been. Once truth can be visualized, it can be reached. I tried to do right. The problem is right and wrong are social constraints. Though the saying promises that "the truth will set you free," it doesn't warn that freedom has its costs. The quest to continue the struggle often calls for courage. The courage to withstand the pain, the courage to reject the status quo. The courage to stand alone and face the night. With horror, I recall the times I was told the abuse would die with me if I chose not to be an abuser. "If I choose to do right" were words mumbled by people who couldn't comprehend their cost. I relied on that lie. I never questioned the voices, though they showed the speakers hadn't a clue, though they soothingly said they understood. Still, it was my silence that allowed the abusers to thrive. Abuse must be exposed. Abuse needs to be stopped.

I have heard that everyone who sits to write draws from personal experiences. People choose events to elaborate on glimpses of what they've seen or the people they've been. I'll give my account mingled between the lines of what time has helped me to accept as "poetic justice."

Dad wanted my name to be Jackson, after his father's. However, a family of strangers seldom share details of importance. At Dad's burial, mom and other living family members discovered Jackson to be his father's name. This was found while reading his father's gravestone as I was being given his family's history by one of his remaining brothers. I never was able to know my dad's family because of circumstances beyond my control. So, Dad's brother explained how I would have been related to the people whose names were on the stones in the family cemetery. I remember liking what some of the old markers said. Old Southern tombstones don't mix words. They told who the person was without incorporating political correctness. At the time, I was old enough to know that glimpses from the past appear at the least opportune moments to kick you. Mom received her kick when she figured out the reason behind dad's choice of names for me. The saying is, "No good deed goes unpunished." My name is Jackson in this account because of Dad's request.

I had what others watching from a safer distance might call a normal childhood. From it, I recall events with laughter and tears. I remember being called from the fields, which roll through the memories of my youth. The neighborhood kids used to run and play, kick the can, and hide-n-seek in those fields. I recall the reality of having to return when the cool evening breeze began to blow. Though, I could not rest and forget the sweltering heat of a few hours prior. I recall returning to the house soon after lightning bugs came out. I remember watching a well-dressed man sitting in his rocking chair, acting like he knew who we were. I recall him talking like he'd leave his chair to sit at our table any moment. I remember the day when that horrible scream was heard throughout the world. That day, all children were called in. That day, the man who owned the rocking chair was shot. Shot twice while riding through Dallas. He was sitting in a long black car. I remember him being killed while reaching for a dream called "Camelot." I recall waiting for an explanation. None has been found. I remember the next person to take his place, but the rocking chair, the man, and Camelot are gone. All that remains are scattered images branded in a child's mind.

I recall going into the house announcing my return from kindergarten and grandma asking if I would like soup for lunch. My answer was, "Nope. The house is on fire." I spoke those words while running across the porch to cross the street. I was going to my friend's house. We were going to sit on her steps and watch that house burn. Mom soon followed. She was crying, carrying our dog. She had to return to the house when my friend's mom asked, "Where's your baby?" I recall watching grandma through the window as she sat in her chair, one with herself, in a house full of flames. She was relaxed, as though flames and smoke were normal. I recall listening to the roar of the fire trucks coming up the street. How those men jumped off before the trucks stopped. They ran into the house, fire blazing and hoses in hand, flooding the place. I recall wondering why the smoke was changing colors and grandma sitting in its midst, at peace with a house on fire.

That day, the firemen didn't have time to wave or talk like they did when we saw them passing our school. That day did not permit the standard pleasantries. I still liked the firemen, even though they didn't let me jump into their jumping ring when I escaped from the teacher and climbed the school's flagpole. That day, the day I recall as the house's first fire, the firemen jumped from their trucks, ran into the house, and put out that fire. However, they were unable to convince grandma to leave her throne.

I recall grandma ranting on her favorite topic. "Man has never walked on the Moon." Grandma refused to believe any news report on the subject because she saw the coverage of what it would look like and then saw it live. That instant, she jumped to her feet, stomping, yelling, "They've used the same footage." "They just want people to believe they've sent a man to the moon to have the ability to raise our taxes." she'd proclaim to her captured audience. While we ran and ducted, trying not to be slugged by her thrusting arms. To think these words came through the lips of the woman who believed every word those lying weathermen said.

"Some people ask that we give them control of our lives," she'd warn, "because theirs's is out of control."

My name is Jackson; born in the land where we hold these truths to be self-evident.

Raised under the constant threat of losing them.

The whole system is filled with people who have authority,

Yet not one of them stands accountable.

There are a few things of which I am sure:

People who stand proclaiming they're in charge aren't.

A screaming person seldom says anything.

People without voices have no rights.

From a distance, the overview of my youth may appear like that of your average Jackson. My account, however, should have you wondering if our pictures have been colored with the same crayons.

Chapter 2

I was in a field I cared for on the other side of the country when my cell phone rang. It was the new voice of someone from my past. A call to inform me of an event. A call that reminded me where I came from. A call to tell me that, finally, someone I was once acquainted with had been taken into custody. A call that informed me one of the family's children's molesters had been uncovered.

The years vanished. The distance between myself and the house failed. My escape had been foiled. I was immediately transported back to the house. I was forced to realize that I could never escape the abuses. I gathered the tattered bits and pieces of myself and carried them with me. Though alone again, I knew I could not remain invisible.

One of the damming things about abuse is that you are trained to remain silent. Abuse teaches you not to show feelings. Forgive me when I forget to express my soul's inner workings. This torture is usual for an abused person, and we assume everyone understands how our abuses force our silence. But silence will not allow its victims to escape. I stood in that field, silent, trying to suppress my pains. A heart will cry, or the soul will suffer the consequences.

"Can you believe it?" she said. I discovered through the hint of a smoker's voice who was on the other end.

I always thought that whenever I arrived at that moment, I would be permitted to say, "I told you." At that moment, I felt the torture of children being victimized and unable to stop their suffering. Past predictions no longer mattered. During that moment, I started realizing the torments I suppressed.

"They have him in jail and get this; they are investigating how this type of thing could happen." She explained.

I listened to her uncontrolled excitement as I asked myself, "Who will help the children?"

My mind returned to a night from my youth, continuously being branded into the folds of my being. Darkness was beginning to fall. I heard his car. We four kids ran with all our might to the house, screaming to warn each other. Four kids scrambling their way into their planned escapes. Four kids, hiding, listening through the forced silence. Four kids wondering which one would be discovered? I wished this would be my night, but I accepted that it likely would fall to another. Was Dad happy or in a bad mood? Would tonight bring money or punishment? Would there be a need to buy new lamps, would flying ashtrays leave indentations and abrasions in us? Whichever mood it was, he was returning, and Mom would be armed.

I stayed silently in my box, hidden amongst the other boxes, tucked away in our attic room. I'd like to know how long I was there. My memory has nothing happening outside the attic room. Nothing else could be heard other than what sounded like the boxes' heartbeat. I cannot recall screaming, crying, or laughing. Nothing was moving. No light came shining through the handle hole warning of the doors opening. Often, I have wondered what I heard because my mind refuses to let me know. Why, in this memory, is the world overcome by silence?

Ours was a big old farmhouse. Supposedly built to keep its occupants safe. It was finished around the turn of the century. It was complete with a horse barn and carriage garage. It was a nice-looking house, though it always appeared to be out of place. Like it had been scooped up from someplace in the south and planted across the border. It had a basement with a smaller room for coal before the gas furnace was installed. Dad and I cleaned that room. We built shelves for its walls so car parts could be stored. When I was a kid, mechanics fixed cars. It was unheard of to go to an auto parts store and pull some new parts from the shelf. If dad and I could not fix something, we would climb in the truck, go to the junkyard, and find one we could work with. To put a new part in an old car was unacceptable. It had something to do with new wine in old bottles. I had heard dad tell others it was about American pride. When I was a kid, what people built was built to last. To not fix a broken part or replace a damaged part with something from a shelf would have caused a glorious rebellion. The whole darn thing would have blown apart.

I stayed in the safety of my box, hidden amongst other containers filled with other unwanted, forgotten items. There were boxes filled with seasonal clothing and boxes of pots-n-pans. The first half of the attic room was filled with boxes like mine. My box had nothing to distinguish it from the others. I stayed still as my mind raced through the events of my existence. For a moment, I was reeling from the thought of not being discovered for the first time. However, the problem I could not get past was the mind of a soon-to-be fourth grader is seldom content with self-praise. Did seeking the acceptance of a victory cause me to depart the box?

I tiptoed across the attic room. I snuck through what was once called the boy's room. I crept down the stairs, carefully avoiding the steps that would announce my arrival. I turned the corner of the last few steps. There, upon our Early American couch, they sat. They are being my two brothers and little sister. At first, I thought they had been caught. Until I remembered that only one of them was capable of being beaten. They all sat with their mouths wide open and stared into the kitchen. Not a sound left their throats, though their mouths were hinged open. Who were these kids sitting on mom's couch? It was an eerie sight, although a scene grandma had often painted. She warned us such places existed in other houses across the nation, but I never imagined the lack of sound could suck the color and life of children.

Grandma was not there. She worked nights. My older sister, the oldest kid in our household of eight, was away at college. Not even the dog dared to bark. I had nothing to warn me.

I looked.

Dad was on one side of the closet door we used for a can pantry,

Mom hung from the other, her feet just a few inches off the floor. Her legs kicked in the air as her body tried to find a rhythm. She must have been trying to break through my silence. I can still see the rope on the side of her neck, but in the front, it wasn't viewable because it was buried in the soft folds of her flesh. Her flesh had changed colors. It had a green hue, turning dark blue though her lips were purple.

I don't know to this day why I don't recall sounds or why those colors are so vivid in my mind. The scene did not look anything like the hangings on TV.

I don't know how I do, but I recall the TV was on, though I don't remember what was on it. It was a Thursday, but I cannot remember what I did next. I've been told I screamed. I have been told I ran into the kitchen and hit Dad. The fact remains I can't remember and probably never will. At some point, I jumped off the long country-style porch, which I proudly watched Dad rebuild only a few weeks earlier. As he built our new front porch, it struck me that he was clever to use the best of the old lumber to close in the side and create a door so the space could be used for storage and hiding.

Next, I recall jumping on the neighbor's porch and looking through the door's glass while trying to beat it down. I was searching for a sign of life in their home. When I viewed the neighbors coming down their stairs. His hairy legs were coming out of his boxers. His wife was following, dawning a faded flower-printed threadbare housecoat. Before they could descend, I barged in.

People did not lock their doors when I was a kid. She started to scold me while trying to use the sentence. "Just who do you think...?"

I never thought she liked us. We used to pass our football in our yard. Other kids would come, and we'd play football. Her husband would come out and practically beg us to not play there. It was our yard, so we ignored him. At least, we did until the day someone tipped the ball, and it crashed through a big plate glass window. Before we could scatter, he was out on their kitchen's landing, inviting us for a meal. We tried to explain how busy we were. At that moment, I could think of several things I needed to accomplish. He insisted. We painstakingly meandered into their home. His family was seated around a vast Quaker-style oak table. Nothing was on the stove in pots and pans. Each dish had its own bowl or platter. And each had its place on their table. In the center of the table was a huge bowl of homemade chicken soup. In it was the football my brother once owned. Each of us gathered about and ate whatever was placed on our plates. I was prepared to tell her what a good cook she was, but the occasion never presented itself. I was afraid if I spoke, they'd ask about the ball. I don't recall anyone touching the soup despite its bountiful supply.

Not that first word was spoken concerning their broken window. I can assure you no one from the game noticed the football. When the meal was finished, their kids cleared the table as she stood her station at the sink washing the dishes. He took the clean dishes from the rack and, finished drying them, and then returned them to their proper place. They continued to do this until we found a good enough reason to be released. He then excused himself to walk us to the door. She followed, never made a sound, but we knew she followed. Though he escorted us, it was clear he was with her. Not a thing was said concerning that incident. To her dying day, Mom may not have known what happened to my brother's football. Through the years, I've wondered if those neighbors lived that way. Their bread had a dish. Not the first order was issued. They each knew their tasks and fulfilled their missions. They lived in a house where everyone had their part. Was this meal a show to brand the details of an image into my mind? He was a good but strange man; my oldest sister hated his guts.

One day, when they first came to our neighborhood, he saw me out on my bike, which didn't have a seat. A few days later, he called me over and invited me into their garage. A new bike seat was hanging from a ceiling joist next to the double plate. It still had the bike shop's price tag on its dust-free cover. He explained why he no longer needed it while lowering it from an old nail. He then started adjusting things about my bike and oiling the chain after adding the seat. He had me take it for a spin; admittedly, the man did excellent work.

He would come out on their porch at about one o'clock each afternoon to smoke his pipe. He would sit with his wife and talk. He was mainly a soft-spoken, sweet tea-drinking, two-fried eggs with three strips of bacon and dry toast, quiet man. Until it came to cleaning his pipe. After he had meticulously packed it just right and smoked it for a while, he would scrape its bowl and beat it against the porch's top handrail. It sounded like a judge pounding his gavel.

He worked nights at the airport. So, he and his wife frequently reminded us to keep our noise below a roar until one O'clock. He needed his sleep. The entire time they lived there, that man watched over me. He often came over to talk to my oldest sister about something she'd done. His son and I were friends. I think the man sort of liked me. He looked out for the kids in my household. I saw him descending the stairs in his boxers before I burst into their living room. I somehow managed to blurt out, "Dad's killing Mom." His speed made superman look like he was standing still. Their kids started to come down to see what the noise was. His wife grabbed me from behind and spun me around as she told me I couldn't leave her. She did this while demanding that their kids go back to their beds. She was hugging me tightly. She explained to me that I needed to stay. She had forgotten who I was, and her motherly instincts took over. We stood in the center of their living room while she held me in her embrace, rubbing my back. She rocked me back and forth, though occasionally, she patted me. I was being treated in a manner that loving mothers usually reserve for their child who is terribly ill. This probably stands out because I can't recall when my mom said she loved me or hugged me, and now a woman who did not care for me was showing me she loved me.

The cops came. I do not know who called them. One of them was in the house for a long time. Still, the neighbor's wife wouldn't let me go. When the cop came out, we went to their porch. The neighbor man followed Mom, who was following the cop. The neighbor was rubbing mom's shoulders. The neighbor was dressed in my memory as he followed her, but I can't recall him getting dressed. When they came to the street, they stopped. There, the cop could examine mom's neck. The cop told Mom she would need to find places for us to stay that night. I never saw Dad in the house again after the hanging, but once. Dad must have picked Grandma up that night because I have been told she stayed in the house with him.

I remember that only one of the cops ventured from their car. The other stayed halfway in and out of the cruiser. Like he was ready to leave at a moment's notice. I occasionally heard rumors about dad and his dealings with the law officers. It didn't go so well for them that night. It was rumored that dad sold the county's finest corn from mason jars.

I am still struggling with where the others family's member went. I believe my oldest brother went to a friend's house in the country, and mom and my baby sister went to my aunt, whose husband served another tour in Viet Nam. My brother and I went to grandma's baby brother's place. They had a pinball machine. I am younger, so I watched my brother play pinball that night as my great-aunt served me cold sodas. Then, we skipped school and hung out with my great uncle. My brother, great uncle, and I played hooky. We had a blast. When the weekend was over, so was our escape. We had to be returned. Dad only came after the divorce was final to get a few things and start cleaning our used parts room. I was at the river fishing. He did not take all the stuff the judge told him he could. He only got a few things that mom said he could have.

After the divorce, Dad would come by on weekends for a little while. He'd show up at the curb about one o'clock, and my oldest brother, who has special needs, and my little sister and I would climb in his car to get candy or ice cream with him. He was trying to say he loved us and was sorry for the mess. These visits did not last long. Dad was too busy dying. For him, death was a slow process. It started at birth. It emerged again to speed into a maddening pace after the sinking of the Navy ship he was on during WWII. It ended with the raising of his glass.

Mom warned us that there would be changes as we returned to the house. We were given what she called "new rules." I didn't particularly care for the old ones, so I listened carefully for a ray of hope which might be found in the new. No such luck. Same darn rules, except Dad or strangers couldn't come in. Which was a crazy rule. We couldn't have friends in our house. We could not even answer the door for him or strangers. Dad was no longer welcome. Still, I never heard mom say a bad word concerning him. Though her family seldom had a nice one to repeat. Still, I remember those flying ashtrays, her beating him with lamps, the refusing to cook for or sleep with him. I remember the fights over the lesser queen dropping off her daughter. (When she was born, her mother left her at the hospital for her mother to rescue) she came along with any other her mother could pawn off.) I remember plenty, and to think many claims my scars aren't visible. After their divorce, mom cleaned houses, took in laundry, and did sewing projects for the wealthy to scrape enough up for our survival. Later she got a job at the factory, cleaned houses, took in laundry and sewed for the rich, and worked at the factory in her spare time.

Grandma warned us, "People would be coming to ask questions." We were not to tell them a thing. Those people wanted to take us. We did not want to know what happened to children removed by the authority. "If we thought it was hard where we were, we didn't know a thing." She'd often rant while beating us, "Go ahead, open your mouths and get taken. You'll be in for a rude awakening."

One day, when I returned from school, one of those child takers tried to question me through the house door. Why would I talk to anyone like that? He came in his highly polished wingtip shoes, white stiff starched shirt, skinny tie, and pencil neck. His hair was slicked back, and his beady eyes were looking for a sign of movement behind the door. He kept looking at his notepad for questions he thought I was bound to answer. This guy was the authority Grandma had warned about. That man didn't know beans about me or the other kids in the house. He didn't think we were raised by experts in using shadows. He just kept asking, "Is there food in the house?" Not have you eaten. "Does your mom treat you right?" instead of How'd you get those marks on your back and upper legs. "Does she ever spank you?" Not have you been knocked out by their spankings? Have you been spanked by an electric cord, skillet, belt, cook spoon, ball-bat, or stabbed by an icepick? Have you ever been beaten awake or kicked and jumped on for lying on the floor even though you weren't allowed on the living room's furniture? I don't know what he was thinking, trying to get one of us to give him a reason to take us.

Usually, or when I returned from school on time, I rode with Mom as she drove Grandma to work. Then she'd work in the basement if she had no house to clean. There was another time when I came late when one of those state-issued strangers came strolling up our walk like he owned the thing. I slipped the dog out the back when he got near the porch's steps. That man could run, jump the gate in stride, and never return. Grandma warned that they'd try to trick us.

Some adults never asked questions. Some pointed at me while explaining to others what they claimed I was. Those of the latter group seem to never stop talking. Divorces were uncommon when I was a kid. Those pointing fingers talkers tried to hide their lying lips, which spoke harsh words about me as though my ears couldn't hear. Other people would yell and carry on, trying to humiliate me if I'd let them. I heard them. At school, I had to go with the official questionnaires every so often. They would ask a lot of questions. I really refused to answer, though I gave answers. It may sound strange, but I never realized how bad I had it until they explained it.

They wanted to know if I caused the divorce.

They wanted to know if I caused my dad to get arrested.

I was a kid leaving the third grade.

I did not give Dad the rope.

I was hiding.

I did not tell Mom to leave him.

I was a kid.

I went to our makeshift babysitter's and swam from the opening until the pool's closing.

I did not tell Mom things I knew.

I never mentioned a thing about the still under the barn outside of town.

I did not tell Dad had a girlfriend.

I knew things that Mom might have wanted to know.

I kept my mouth shut just like Grandma told me.

I was a kid trying to ride my bike, swim at the community pool, and find a friend. I was a kid being framed by adults outside my family who were Mom's family members. Those monsters did not like us. They only pretended to like me in front of others so they could take from me. I was tired of being told that I had a black half-sister. Why didn't they pick her up and bring her over? I would have played with her. I was tired of being told what a low life I was for causing the divorce. I was a kid trying to find the way in a world of people who were not who or what they were supposed to be. I did not cause Dad to get arrested. Trying to hang Mom was entirely his idea. Who knew it would be the straw that broke the camel's back? I had seen other wives, mostly my aunts (the monster ones), who had been beaten, and they took their husbands back before they were released from their cells.

Most of the time, our household of strangers came together because of tragedies. The mindless daily grind of our goalless existence placed the flame on our world.

It is a fact Mom did get her divorce, but I know nothing of Dad ever being arrested.

The cops came looking for him once. They did not find him. It was before the hanging, and as far as I know, whatever was wrong seems to have faded after we visited the man with the still beneath his barn.

I was a kid trapped in a world of questioning adults who only needed half the information to arrive at a full conclusion. Only a few adults seemed able to remember what it was like to be a kid. The strange man next door was pretty good at pulling it off occasionally. He would accidentally prove he knew.

When his son and I would get into a fight. Which happens regularly to relieve ourselves from the boredom of being poor. The man would tell us to go to their fringe and choose our eggs. We were to walk around the block, squeezing the eggs lengthwise between our palms. If we were still mad when we returned, we could throw our eggs against his maple tree.

We'd be laughing before we made the first corner. Jogging as soon as we were out of sight. We were tired of running when we got to that last bend, only to have our full anger reappear and return in time for that final stretch. When we were spotted, the area behind the maple cleared. I can report that not one egg survived and that maple trees thrive on eggs.

It is odd to think of; our block was horseshoe-shaped. Nothing about the house was like it was supposed to be.

Chapter 3

The call from my past had me wondering. Who will help the children? As a plethora of thoughts raced through my brain. Its maddening being the survivor of child abuse. You never escape. It is true you may suppress it, but life has its ways of bringing up and forcing you to live with your past. People ask simple questions, but your mind takes you through numbing events, which you must filter before responding. You must in a certain manor, or be your differences will be discovered. We live in a society which demands normalcy, yet no one is normal.

At the house, there are three types of people: the abusers, the enablers, and the victims. The danger lies in discovery. Who is what is made more difficult at any time because the members exchange rolls from time to time to keep their prey on their toes? No one stays in one group. Our parts change places for survival from time to time, which adds to the torture.

My account is not chronological, but life needs to be grasped; this may not occur in chronological order. The order of events might take a lot of work to follow. This might be a warning. We are doing something terribly wrong while expecting different outcomes. Besides, my mind cannot relate to the events in chronological order. When I tell my story, I must do so in increments because to give the account, I must relive them. This is disturbing because I know the order of events, yet I cannot alter the outcomes. I also know that science says which each telling I must stray further from the truth.

The smoker's call informed me of the arrest of my cousin once removed. It was the knowledge that some things can never be made right. There are some curves some wrinkles men will never straighten. Their remains are memories from a child wandering the streets, naive enough to believe, "All men are created equal." That all mankind was given by God the rights to life, liberty, and the pursuit of happiness. We mustn't "let it be forgotten that once there was a spot, for one brief shining moment, known as Camelot." Her call, time, and the distance arrested me through the fallacy concerning the abusive lifecycle dying with me if I would not become an abuser.

There is something terribly wrong concerning that thought process. I had never considered the nameless faces of children who suffered because I had chosen to remain silent. Unwittingly, I had allowed myself to be an enabler. I had permitted my unexpressed fears to let me stay silent. There remains something incomplete in that thought process that enables the comforts of deception. The lie is, "I am only accountable for my actions." The horrible things I've allowed the monsters or their offspring to perform during my silence are not only their problems. Something is wrong with the thinking; it encourages silence when there should be screams. The abused must force themselves to be heard.

Her call caused me to realize my hands could never be cleaned if I permitted myself to remain silent. My mind immediately went to the reality that I would someday have to return to the house. Others have claimed their longest journeys begin with a step. Mine started with that thought. Still, most of the abusers I once thought I knew have died. I admit good and evil abide in everyone. The difference is one of the degrees. Water is hot at two hundred-eleven degrees; at two hundred and twelve, it begins to boil and becomes steam. Steam has powered machines that have moved mountains. The house is part of my heritage. Mom's lawyer has not handled her wishes as she requested in her will. The thieves have come running. Soon, even these events will be passed.

A thousand times, I have seen myself standing outside the house. Surrounded by confused people concerned about what I was doing. My mind allows the past and the future to come crashing together with such a force; if I am not careful, they will rob me of tomorrow. The events have opened my eyes to the fact that the houses evil will worm its way back into my mind. I could take you to my street and tell you evil resides at the house; you would sense the correct structure.

Chapter 4

Mom and Dad's divorce was finalized, but mine never came. The queens have woven their webs. Still, to this day, if I hear grandmas' voice while sleeping, I awaken. She had a way that no one could understand. Rumor was that grandma and her youngest daughter once lived together with their men at the close of WWII. I was warned to never ask questions about that again. I haven't heard much, and existence has taught me to not speculate.

I know the queens can do things no other is permitted to do. (The Queen is what grandma became when I became punishable. The lesser queens are her favored daughters and the favorite granddaughters. I will not disclose their names because history should forget them.) It is acceptable for them, but it's not for others. They'll taunt. "You had your father arrested." "You caused your parents' divorce." "You have a black sister." Every time I tried to stand; I was beaten down. My brother was a gentler, quieter soul. The court permitted him to leave after a few years of struggling. That way was not opened for me. I remember him knocking on the door, waiting on the porch to get his part of the child support checks.

Today, truth is funny.

I have often heard it will set you free.

I have a few questions.

Can truth do it on its own?

Mustn't truth be embraced?

Can truth truly change and remain truthful?

Might our perception of truth have more control than truth?

Things that were never a part of me were thrust into me. "You are no good and will end up like your father." "Look at the bull; look at the snot fly." Simple statements used to disgrace. It was as though the queens needed to humiliate others so they could appear happy upon their miserable thrones. Some people cannot appear satisfied until they've made others suffer more misery than they perceive themselves to be in.

I suspect it's easier to go through existence accepting others' answers than to think for yourself. When Dad would come to pick us up, my one brother refused to go. I never asked why. I've heard he caught Dad with the other woman, which is why he was beaten. I heard it led to the fight and Mom's hanging. I had to endure a lot of talks. I heard Dad was a drunk, but I still remember when the Queen, who did most of the talking kids, needed food or shoes, she'd go to him. I heard he was good for nothing, but it always seemed to change their story when their cars were broken.

Dad rebuilt cars in our horse barn. I remember how he brought home a puppy because its mother wouldn't feed her runt. I heard of Moms crying and carrying on about not wanting a dog until Dad pulled it out of his jacket pocket. I heard he stopped by the drugstore to get an eyedropper so Mom could feed it. I heard how she made the dog's bottles as she prepared mine. I also remember my dog thought he belonged to mom. I've been told Dad ran shine. But I've never seen a drop of alcohol touch his lips. We could not say darn or shucks in grandma's presence because heathens used those words. I know she kept part of a bottle of Black Velvet in her closet, which she'd sip daily to cure her of snow snake infections. I also understand those who did the talking had secrets of their own. I know none of us are normal. All of us have issues. It's hard and often dangerous to figure people out. Good people do bad things, and bad people stumble into doing something right.

Dad would come about one o'clock in the afternoon every other Saturday, but only for a short while. My oldest brother, little sister, and I would ride through the country with our candy or go get our ice cream with him. The top of his car would be down. The wind would be blowing my hair, and I was as free as the wind made my hair in that moment. If it were candy, we would stop at a little country store down the way, but on another street. He allowed us to eat one piece of candy as soon as it was purchased. The rest we had to take home. Ice cream was eaten in front of the dairy on the rollers the dairymen used to load their trucks. We ate all our ice cream before re-entering Dad's car. I did not realize that ice cream that would be the best store-bought ice cream I'd ever have.

I tried to get to know Dad but was too young to learn to investigate the care he gave his cars. Dad kept his cars up. They were classics. He would get a vehicle and thoroughly go through it. The car buffs in town said he was the best body man around. Grandma would look out to see him and his cars, then report, "The devils in the details." He would return us to the house at the end of his allotted time. I would slowly slide out. Then he would drive off. The lesser Queen's kids, "my cousins," would run from the house. Before we arrived at the rebuilt long porch, I once admired Dad for rebuilding. Their mother would take our candy and give them (under the pretense of sharing). Dad would be gone once again, and I would be none the wiser, trapped in a world that never wanted me. After spending two or three hours with the man, I was saddened because I did not know who he was.

Chapter 5

Whenever the Army transferred my uncle, he and his family would come to stay with us. It was crowded in the house, more so then. Then, the house had too many cooks and not enough bathrooms, but I loved it. They could only stay a week or two, but I looked forward to their return as soon as I saw them pile in their car and head out for some Fort. When my uncle and Aunt stayed with us, nothing happened. It appeared they always came in the middle of the night. On those nights, we were all awakened and ate BLTs. We stayed up talking and listening to the adults. My uncle would play with us, and my aunt would encourage me by listening. She listened so intensely to whatever it was I told her. We always stayed up too late when they came and never went to school the next day.

Even dad seemed to look forward to their arrival.

When they were at our house, the monsters stayed away, and the ones in the house had to remain camouflaged. If, by chance, one of those out-of-house monsters felt like they needed to talk with my uncle, he would drive to them. I loved it when my uncle and aunt came. It was like the rest of existence; good things mingled with sinister truths camouflaged by lies. Still, when they arrived, the monsters had to behave.

I have been told I used to shake my leg and sing Hound Dog when Elvis was on the radio. I have been told I threw a board from an old picket fence we took down, and the board I threw hit my brother in his eye. I have been told that is why he needed glasses. I thought dad had taken him to the hospital to have a splitter removed. I was not in school when this happened, so I must have been three or four. Like the others, I was trying to help throw the old pickets into the trash pile. I had trouble believing I purposely hit or hurt him. Still, I carried the guilt of hurting my brother for years until I found out it never happened. My brother's astigmatism caused him to need glasses. He was not taken to the hospital. They went to the eye doctor. I was told several times how I was afraid of my uncle's wife because she'd kill Americans while they slept. I wonder why all those who remembered this did not remember who told a three-year-old that German women killed Americans while they slept. Lucky for me, I remember who told me how afraid I was of the aunt who took me in.

Like most kids, I remember the things in my room transformed by darkness. I remember being yelled at to stop making that ruckus and to get to sleep. I remember listening to the noises outside and watching the imaginary images as I tried to lay perfectly still. I remember trying to stay up to defend myself from them and then silently laughing at myself for trying to outstare the things they'd returned to as daylight came. I remember them introducing me to others and then telling them stuff they said I'd done while warning them of what I'd do. This was done so that they could quickly discredit me if I told them.

I realize that I see my uncle and aunt through borrowed eyes. When it comes to them, I have older eyes. I have felt the warmth of their repeatedly stopping, stooping to help me. I knew the house was on guard when they were with us. I knew they would keep us safe.

Have you ever noticed how a man asks a girl to be his bride? Yet it takes years of living and existence to make her one? Once kids have gone and the years have furrowed their faces, a few men light up at the thought of their wives. It is their life experiences together that have transformed her into his bride. I understand this because the very idea of my aunt and uncle comforts me.

Odd to think of the people who are there for you when you're being raised by the streets.

My uncle was called upon to do another tour in Vietnam. I was safe with my aunt, and she allowed the world to know it. She moved into an apartment four miles from our school but was in the wrong direction from the house. When school was out, I'd walk to their apartment a lot. Their two girls got home after I'd been there a little while because they went to a private school. When I finally had to return to the house, I would be talked to. Not one of the standard talking; one of those you get while they are trying to beat information in.

"Jackson, I don't want you to go there; she doesn't want you around."

The problem was, they couldn't convince me. I had eyes of my own. My aunt would smile when I showed up. Her crow's feet were beginning to show. When she smiled, it was real, not one of the smiles the monsters used to try and trick me. She'd talk to me like one of her kids. Even I could not leave her alone if my flirtatious uncle came over. She did not like being chased by him.

I seldom accept things solely because someone said it was so. I am hard-headed. I must find out on my own. It may be because I've suffered from so many lies.

"An inquisitive mind," some say.

"Bullheaded" is what the queens branded me with.

"The boy never shows a sign of hearing; he just sits there and ignores everything." I wonder if they thought my acting out was purely coincidental.

We could walk the same streets, go to the same places, and still view the world from different perspectives.

The Queen would swear, "It never happened." It did; she just didn't know where to look.

For instance, at the weddings, they would sit and strain to see one of her monsters (the perpetual isle walker) every time she attempted to become someone's bride; she wore a white dress. The Queen's mother claimed her to be the main attraction. I was patient, knowing she would show up, but not until that song played. I watched the grooms. He was the nervous guy up front. I liked to see him when he got his first glimpse of her. His eyes, catching that first glimpse of her, told the tale. Those men had good cause to be scared.

My guardian Aunt would laugh with me. She would slip in through her apartment's back door and make our chocolate pudding on the stove, with milk. We would talk. When my aunt listened, it was like I was saying the only words which mattered. She would get after us and laugh at us for playing in the ditch that flowed behind their apartment. "Jackson, what is then with you? Do you know what that then is?" she'd enquire.

I would get it when I returned to the house, but I always returned to my aunt's.

At our house, kids ate whatever we could sneak and fix; or we'd suffer through whatever was prepared after the monsters had doctored it. That stuff was no longer fit for human consumption. Sometimes, I would eat it anyway, but I'd get sick at night and have to go to school with an upset stomach. Sometimes, I feel I owe my life to "Campbell's Chicken Noodle Soup." My food allotment for the week was six cans of Campbell's Chicken Noodle Soup, 1 bag of Chip Ahoy cholate chip cookies, and a small glass of milk per eating of cookies. (Breakfast) sometimes, the cookies were exchanged for a box of Captain Crunch. Sometimes, we'd get a hunk of trail bologna. Grandma would grid it up and make what we called bologna salad. I got in trouble more than my share of times for sneaking a sandwich from it. It wasn't that there wasn't food in the house; it wasn't our food. It was for when the visiting monsters and their kids came or for putting on that we were the all-American family, not for our everyday consumption.

Chapter 6

Not every memory from the house is terrible, though some now can wake me. I am still determining the year, but it would probably be sixty-three or sixty-four. Mom had just gotten hired and was the first woman to work in the new factory that the man who controlled the industry in our town owned. One of the guys at the factory told her if she were to varnish watermelons, they would keep all winter if they were kept cool.

We were going to Kentucky for my Great Uncle's family reunion. We used to go to grandma's family reunions, but they didn't like us, so we just switched family reunions. Anyway, Melons were cheaper in Kentucky. Every year, we went to Kentucky for two weeks to help with the harvest, clean, and have fun. This would be Labor Day weekend for the rest of America. Amongst the snakes and varmints of Kentucky, I felt safe. There, our extended family looked after us. The family monsters had to be on their best behavior, or the truth would ooze out. People would come from all around the country. Tables made from sawhorses and sheets of plywood line the yard. They would be bursting with good food. Kids ran and played while the adults sat talking about things adults talk about.

I loved to chase the chickens and was told if I caught one, I could do anything I wanted to with it. I love fried chicken.

On the way back to the house, we stopped at a field where two farmhands were selling melons at a roadside shack. We had two carloads of fresh watermelons when we pulled out. They were on our laps, on the floor, and filling the trunks. Mom and I were happy. She was so happy she forgot to mind the speed limit until the red lights showed up. She received her first ticket. We went off to pay for the thing. Cops in Kentucky would not accept payment like ours did, but even that ticket couldn't dampen her spirit. They took her money at the courthouse, and we kept our melons. She knew where to stop to get varnish, as we dreamed of eating melon at Christmas.

Christmas was a big deal at the house. We'd get a bushel of what Grandma called Washington Apples, though they were picked from an orchard nearby. A box of Florida oranges and one of the tangerines that Grandma would order from the man who delivered produce to the restaurant where she cooked. She would take our fruit to make her fruit salad. It would be complete with our fresh fruit, canned pineapple, pears, peaches, all the juices, and a big jar of cherries and walnuts.

Then the relatives would come. They ate piles of our gift and left only a small bowl for us. That was only done because they couldn't fit it in the containers they brought, or they would have taken it also. These low-life thieves seemed to leave in time to avoid cleaning the holiday mess I was destined to be informed we'd made. They came over to get their presents and destroyed ours.

That year, our Christmas was going to be the best ever. We would be eating watermelon after they left. It gave me something to smile about, even when I remembered how those kids scampered like rats to hide their toys when we had to go to their houses. I knew I would be eating watermelon after they finally left. They could break my toy. They could devour or destroy our nourishment; in my mind, the line had been drawn; they could not eat our watermelon. It no longer mattered what they did. After they left, I would eat watermelon.

Mom rose from sleep at about one o'clock every morning to begin doing people's laundry. By five-thirty, she was well into her second pot of percolated coffee and was moving out the door on her way to the factory. I remember grandma making mom switch brands of coffee because grandma felt sorry for that poor, overwork man from the commercials having to pick the perfectly ripe beans by hand.

Some of the bigwigs in town hired mom to clean their homes and do their washing, ironing, sewing, and baking of holiday pies.

Mom worked hard and was seldom permitted the luxury of learning to enjoy cooking. Even so, she had one meal: Fried chicken, real mashed potatoes, homemade milk gravy, cathead biscuits, and fresh corn on the cob. To top this, she would make coconut cream pies, which usually came with banana cream pies. I liked my pie without the baked, wiped egg white stuff on top. This from-scratch feast would stick to your ribs. I enjoyed that meal a lot, but I loved

Mom's pies. Never been much of a cake person, except for my aunt's German chocolate cake. She called them "chocolate cake," and she spread coconut almond icing. I also like pineapple upside-down cake, which is pie, incidentally.

Mom would make all types of pies for special occasions; however, I like only three types: open, closed, and crisscrossed.

Mom would sing to herself in our basement, though others may have confused it with humming. You had to listen closely to be rewarded with the knowledge that she didn't know the words. This is probably why she sang so softly to the rhythm of a song. She must have thought she knew the notes and words at some point. Down in our basement, as the steam from her throat and equipment slowly rose and faded, we were present in form only. In truth, we were upstairs, laughing and carrying on, eating our Christmas watermelon.

The house held its chill. When I got to the house and could hear mom singing, I'd go into the basement. Once there, I'd curl up on the dryer. It was warm. I was snug. Mom kept an old throw rug on it to make it less slippery. These rugs were also for the top of the freezer when we had to turn ice cream. Down in the basement, we were content. Those who came to accuse and proclaim throughout the queendom that I did nothing right would not dare venture into a work area or offer to help.

Even fools know when they've made mistakes. Be a hero and show someone the way to overcome their error.

I recall grandma being told one of her daughters had taken employment. She did not as much as twitch an eyelash. She said she knew it was a lie "because that girl wouldn't take a job as a taster in a pie factory."

I was amused at the Queen's knowledge. However, I was surprised to discover she knew the truth.

After her workday was finished, mom would coat our melons, then chase me off to the bathroom and off to bed. I'd slide between those cold sheets and kick and move about, trying to heat them up until I heard, "You best be getting to sleep up there; cut out that ruckus."

Sometimes, I felt safe in the unguarded basement with its exposed sub pump, wringer washer, steam-presses, and all sorts of steaming outdated contraptions that mom used.

She would talk about when she was a girl. How the trains ran by their house. Sometimes, she'd tell of its stopping to take on water and how a man from the caboose would come to their well and ask for a cool drink.

It was that rich man who'd make any color car you wanted as long as it was black who'd visited them from time to time, she said. I'd heard it said more than once that he'd never appear until someone else came out and threw pennies. Still, he stepped out by himself for a drink of cool water. The way it was told was more in line with Henry not wanting his picture taken unless children were scurrying about his feet. During the depression, the money would have been appreciated. Still, I question it today. Henry, some claim, invented the assembly line. The ones pushing that line have never seen farmer's wives preparing meals during harvest or heard of how Henry became famous by taking away a man's choice.

Mom told how one time three box cars of coal turned over. Some railroad men came to ask grandma if she had a wagon or any way to help in the cleanup. She acted like her mother while telling those men she didn't have a man. Oh! They expressed great sorrow, for some big wigs would ride the train the next day. Grandma tried to lure them in until one of them explained how they would gladly give the coal to anyone who could clean it up before the bigwigs came. Mom said grandma struck the deal and borrowed horses and wagons. She said kids from far and wide came to get the family's allotment of grandma's coal. Not one piece could be found by morning. Grandma mostly almost gave it to family members and sold it to outsiders. The strangers paid the most for it, not knowing what type of woman they were dealing with.

I was told about their dog when she was a kid. He was just an old cur that would wait for their return from school. They were dirt poor. She remembered how they had to eat raw potatoes for weeks and didn't have the means to get a little salt to put on them. She remembered grandma blew their money on a bushel of peaches (This was money her children earned from working.) Grandma controlled all cash in the house again after my sister went to college until me I'd take the beating and keep my money.) These peaches were to be put up to eat when the company came over. Even then, when grandma cooked, adults ate their fill, all company ate with the adults, and the kids of the house starved on scraps together.

She told me about the Railroad. The DT&I (Detroit, Toledo, & Ironton) told how Henry would build his own railroad to deliver his products. All the train bigwigs got together and said to him that if he lay a mile of track outside of Ironton, they'd stop transporting his products.

She talked about things my uncles had done when they were boys. They also skipped school, went fishing, and played football. The oldest was the halfback of his high school's team and still holds records. Though he only played for two years. They skipped school and ran off to join WWII. Both of grandma's sons joined the War at sixteen, and to do so, they willingly lied about their age to escape. Her baby brother was raised mainly by their maternal grandmother until he could run off to the War. He's a half-brother, but no one ever talks about the man who contributed the half. The grandmothers on mom's side were not right. I am unsure why, but for whatever reason, they mistrusted people, men in particular. I remember asking questions once while trying to figure out what it was. Not that I was trying to help. All of them but my grandma was dead. I was trying to figure out why grandma all at once started hating me. There is no logical way to explain the insanity. So many people called things differently that I am still unable to determine the cause. However, I was sure it was a long Latin-sounding word, and the hope of finding a cure was as empty as my spelling the word correctly. I tried to understand why, if Grandma couldn't raise her kids... why did mom trust her with us?

Mom tearfully explained how they rang a bell when her grandfather was murdered.

Mom told how her queen sister of her sneaking off with the boys and smoking corn silks behind the barns. Mom explained that Queen was mean as a snake and didn't care for anyone except herself. Mom told how that lesser Queen married some young boy who shipped off to War, hoping he'd die, so she could collect the money and notoriety. She said when he returned, the lesser Queen was uptown looking for trouble, pushing a married man's baby in her baby carriage. The soldier divorced her. That was the snake that called me everything because my parents had devoiced. Her parents were as well, and apparently, so was she.

Something's seemingly never changed despite their constant changing. I have slowly learned to allow others to grow into who they are instead of torturing myself, wondering why they aren't who I imagined them to be.

Mom would talk about how they were dirt poor. How they wore dresses made of flour sacks. She told how their land was so rocky that it couldn't raise ten pounds of potatoes on twenty pounds of fertilizer. Still, down in the cool, damp basement with her, I imagined myself safe if she sang. For a little while, I was.

I understand from fall to Christmas is a long time for a child, but this period was brutal on Mom. I'm not saying I was not looking forward to those watermelons. I was, but mom was tending to those melons through deferred hope. I was anticipating eating a slice of cool melon with the concurring family pawn, I called mom.

Then, on Christmas day, we awoke. Things were off and running as planned. We flew through the presents, but I didn't receive one, for only some children received gifts in our household. Finally, the company left, and we were preparing to feast on our melons. My concurring Mom came up the basement steps, smiling, carrying the first of our thirty-five glistening watermelons. That thing shined in the stairwell's dingy light like it was still on the vine and covered with morning's dew. It was begging to be devoured.

Soon, the melon knife was poised. We scurried to prepare our plates. When the knife went in, the only thing that came out was liquid and stunk.

We were had. We were well-trained in the art of dejection. Mom's head fell, and her shoulders drooped. It might have been the weight of the knife that caused her to slouch. Not one of us dares notice. The dejection she had draped about her said it all. She looked like she was about to cry, so we busied ourselves, caring out thirty-four other stinking, varnished, overripe, wasted melons. Some of the best jokes are pulled by people who don't stick around to see how bad they got you.

Mom nor I would ever let on. However, occasionally, we would almost permit ourselves to laugh whenever we caught a glimmer of a drop of varnish upon the basement's cool concrete floor. We would never let on how bad that "Jaybird" got us. However, only some things that happened were good.

Chapter 7

One year, for Christmas and my birthday, I was given cutoffs from our hometown lumberyard. I also received a *Handy Andy* tool set and a big box of nails. I spent all awake moments in the basement for days sawing and hammering. I did not allow myself to be disturbed by the occasional threats or yells from those who would not venture into a work area. I made many things; I repaired the middle slat of the bottom landing. I also am the one who broke it when I was being beat one time. I jumped down the complete set of basement stairs to escape, and the weight of my body broke it upon my landing.

Along with my work, I also created a mess. Mom explained to me why we needed to keep our area clean. It could affect the quality of her work. I understood that would jeopardize her income and our food supply. My mind was made up. We agreed we would clean the basement early the following day.

In my defense, I was used to seeing coal and splits from logs placed inside the old cast iron stove. I couldn't understand the operation of the new natural gas furnace. Anyway, when I awoke, I hurried down into the basement. I could hear them talking upstairs about how I went there alone and that it sounded like I was cleaning. The sounds of the praise caused me to do an extra good job.

I had this other uncle. A fix-it uncle. The man could paint a house and not have a drop of paint on him when he finished. Mom would talk over the phone with her sister, and sure enough, her husband (my fix-it uncle) would show up with his toolbox. Mom gave him the title of "The world's best brother-in-law." It's all a matter of perspective because we couldn't leave him alone with my guardian aunt. Mom told her sister how cold our basement was. Our Fixit uncle came over and went straight to work cutting a hole in the big piece of ducting, which fed all the smaller ducting lines to give heat to the basement from the new furnace. It must not have been for me to open and put sawdust, minor scrapes of lumber, and other flammables down.

I felt proud of my accomplishment then screams came from above all at once. It was never good when grandma hollered, you're your full name. I thought I was doing a good thing. I cleaned the basement and used the unwanted materials to help reduce the heating bill.

The firemen came to the house again. Flames were shooting out of the new registers on the first floor about three-quarters the way up the wall. Mom and my fix-it uncle had to repaint the first floor after he repaired the woodwork and the walls.

The meanest and nastiest queen aunt loved to wallpaper, and this opportunity brought her running. Whenever she did something nice for us, we owed her. Such could never be repaid with a single payment. Our debts needed to be often collected over and over for an extended period. I went through the burnt rooms to peel the old chard wallpaper. Mom had to wash those walls and coat them with varnish to lock in the fire smell. I had to sand them quickly so mom could wipe them down to varnish them again. This process was done several times. After this was accomplished, the Queen could supervise the hanging of the wallpaper. I had to help and listen to the Queen's lecturing on my worthlessness. Her leisure conversation with herself concerned her superior technique for hanging wallpaper. Every so often, the Queen departed her throne to mount our little rickety wooden ladder so she could rule the peasants papering the room. She would read the tape measure and call out a number. Mom and my fix-it uncle would cut the paper, paint the glue on its back, and carefully hand it to her as that snake supervised, complained, and directed. She was the only one permitted to know how the papering task needed to be accomplished.

Before any paper was hung, she would study the shadows of a room to determine the direction of the overlapping; she folded the starting piece and started at a corner. Expertly, she'd place her following components at the corner of the wall and ceiling. Then soothingly slid her hand over its surface as others scurried to hand her the brush so she could start brushing out any bubbles or wrinkles. While they were doing this, and when they had just finished, mom repeatedly thanked her for the professional-looking job she had done. I always believed the blooming flowers should have been above the stems. I asked mom. She smiled and said, "O well, it's a little print, and most people will never notice." The truth was, if they did, most wouldn't have the guts to question a queen.

Chapter 8

I was told about how when my grandfather died, he had a quickly drawn will. Because of my grandma's and his divorce, his eldest son is off to War. He willed everything to my aunt. She was supposed to share it with the family. It was just a minor surgery to correct a little hernia, but the doctor made a mistake. It resulted in my grandfather's death. When my aunt received the inheritance, she ran off with two females who said they were friends. They lived the good life. They purchased the finest clothes. They picked up new furnishings for their apartment, and my aunt bought a car. Everything was good until the money ran out, then the friends put her out. My grandfather's estate has nothing left except a ring, a watch, and shaving equipment.

We could usually tell mom anything if we had cleared the way. When mom went off, she'd snapped. There were no warnings; she'd be fine one moment and crazed the next, and still, she could control her crazy when and if she needed to. However, if mom had promised not to punish us for something, she would usually keep it.

One time, my brother decided we would surprise mom by fixing her breakfast. It was before I had started Kindergarten. My brother woke me one morning, and we decided to prepare mom an excellent country breakfast. We waited for her to go outside to hang laundry on the line. When she did, we jumped up and locked her out to keep the surprise. He tripped on the way to the stove. The flying eggs landing made a mess. I was over by the range tossing flower on the table like mom did, but not one of my tossing turned into a single biscuit. The more we tried to clean and help her, the bigger the mess became, until finally, the entire kitchen was one.

I had seen dad push dirt in a hole to pick up the water before setting a post. (I must tell you mom was a neat freak and couldn't stand the sight of a dirty dish. My mom would rotate the ashtrays my uncles used while they smoked to keep her house clean. She was anal about a clean house. Because of our family's roots in the south, grandma never considered a kitchen to be part of any house. Dad never smoked in the house, or the kitchen for that matter.) Anyway, mom never took to things being out of place. We were never permitted to run through our house. In short, our house was spotless. Mom cleaned when she was worried. I knew it was useless to try and find dirt in the kitchen, so I substituted dirt with a little bit of my biscuit's flour. It did not help. The more we tried, the worse it became. Mom saw us through the window and began begging us to let her in. She promised we would not be beaten if we just let her in. Mom confided in us, explaining that we hadn't upset her. She said she just needed to get in so she could start her day. My brother unlocked the door. I was telling him not to trust her. She removed herself from the kitchen window's pane to come to the mudroom's door. She gasped when she came through the mudroom's entry, and her blue eyes shot from her head. She mumbled something to our DEAR LORD WHAT HAD SHE DONE TO DESERVE...

For days mom scrubbed the kitchen bricks to get the flour out of the mortar joints with a toothbrush. I've never received punishment for it. My brother died a few years later. The event is one of those things' mothers recount for others when they share the joys of parenting. She must have been proud of us for figuring out that we could trust her to keep her word. Or she knew if she didn't, we'd never trust her again. I am not saying she never punished us. Because after we hit puberty, everything changed. After puberty, we'd be awakened by beatings or jumped on in our sleep. If we fell to the floor, she'd start kicking our ribs. Mom could be typical one second and madder than a wet hen the next. Who attacks their kids while they're sleeping? That is why I was raised on the streets. The streets were safer than being in the house with Mom, my oldest sister with her stiff bristle brush beating with her bleach and ajax baths. Still, these tortures pail to the tortures of the Queens.

Chapter 9

My day had ended; my supper was eaten. The little ones had gone off to bed. I was sitting back in the *Lazy boy*, remote in hand, ready to watch the Angle game. The phone rang. I received calls for my services; therefore, I answered the phone. My eldest sister was on the other end. We don't talk much. She was almost out of the house when I came along. She tried to raise us while struggling amidst being reared amongst the tortures of the house.

I remember talking with her about the people who'd made a difference in my existence. Some people want to speak to add you to their exciting conversation material. Some talk to keep from thinking, or it's because they like the sound of their voice. Some talk, trying to convince you they know your struggles. The more they talk, the more you realize they don't know. Some hardly talk at all. Often, when they open their mouths, it's just to switch feet. Still, sometimes, from this group, we discover the doers. They're not much on talking, but they do. Somehow, through their fumbling, bumbling to say something just that right way, they open up and reach places in you that words could never find. They haven't come to judge; they've come to help. They can't always say it, but they help lift the burdens. Like the neighbor lady when she forgot I wasn't her child, she allowed her instincts to take over on the night of Mom's hanging.

I do not believe in happenstance. Most of the people my sister said she avoided, I avoided, and the ones who helped her helped me. Most times, I must be careful while talking to my sister. In many ways, she grew up in a different house. She wished to change from being abused to being an abuser. It is odd to talk with my family members. Sometimes, they'll give details they could not possibly know. Sometimes, other family members will take a bow for things I've done. If it was good, they did it. Anything terrible goes to my brother and me. My oldest sister had the uncanny ability to correct me and tell me in great detail things she claimed I had done, though we were both miles from the place. When I accomplished whatever it was, she claimed I did it. It's that same old story. They know the truth but choose to project the lie. They protect the guilty, not caring the innocent must pay. Now that I am older, I think she was raped repeatedly. I remember the person coming from her room, all scratched up, and her running hysterically into the bathroom. I remember plaster falling from the ceiling after hearing the banging of her bedroom wall. I was a small kid and couldn't put it together. Now that I'm older, that rapist is dead, I remember it as a small child, but it's one of the images that has resurfaced to haunt me from time to time.

Once my brother died, I received full credit for all wrongdoings. Death transformed him into a saint. I recognized my sister, but she was in high school when I started school. All she left behind when she went to college was a legacy and a graduation picture on the crocheted doily grandma made. The picture mom placed on the table at the end of the couch. The gift of how well she did everything lingered about the house. Her strong suites were math and science. Mine were abstract thinking. She needed laws and postulants to create parameters. I existed in spaces beyond conventional boundaries; she cashed mom's checks (with grandma) and paid the bills. She could go places because she drove grandma about.

When I came of driving age, mom cashed her own checks and handed the money to grandma to pay the bills. I had to work for spending money. I took grandma someplace once, and she lied about my driving. The next time she sat in my car, she made the mistake of telling me to drive faster. I showed her how to do a bootlegger's turn and power through curves. She told the truth that time, and I never had to take her anyplace again. My sister and I were raised in the same house by different parents, under other forces. We are in different mental hemispheres. She was presented with a mom and a dad, and I was raised around mom by the Queen, her court, that hateful sister, and the street. The Queen was not nurturing to her own children; I never understood why mom trusted her with us?

Though the pillars were periodically painted, the view from the house appeared the same. The changes that the house made were not detectable by human eyes. Still, there were changes, yet they left it in quite the same condition.

"Jackson, have you heard about..." my eldest sister inquired. "This is on the news, everywhere! Even the talk shows are reporting it."

"I have read a few things concerning it off the internet," I replied. "You know the FBI will want to talk with us," I said.

"Jackson, why would they want to talk with us," she said.

"We've escaped; we know them."

'You're right; they will want to talk with us." she mumbled.

"Will you talk with them?" she inquired.

"I will answer their questions," I replied.

"Will they be able to figure it out? She asked.

"I don't think anyone can. If the authorities came close to a realistic answer, they would not like the position it puts them in. They would act as though they had never seen it. This real-life stuff is messy and mutters up the pages of their textbooks." I answered.

"I don't think the others will talk." My sister stated.

"It does not matter if they do. It'll be swept under the carpet to hide it from view, or we will again be ignored because we don't appropriately say things."

I suggested that the family would be afraid to talk. If they were to tell on the others, that member would tell on them. False silence will once again be the vail of self-preservation. By the conversation's end, we would wait to be contacted by the FBI. The next day, she called back to inform us that she had reached out to the FBI. This is a typical situation where the guilty person contacts the authorities to have their part of the crimes covered or forgiven.

Words are such a miserable means of communication. People have stated they wished they lived in that big, beautiful house. Not me. Those people have yet to think it through. Send them to the house. It'll change their minds. Let them live under the dictates of the Queen and her court. The thing which makes the Queen's rule harder to endure is everyone knows she's not perfect. However, few dare to point out her flaws. Like the time they call losing the farm. The Queen fell in love with the younger man, who was also sleeping with her and her thirteen-year-old daughter. This farmhand talked her into selling the farm and then ran off with the money, leaving the two love-struck females to reap vengeance on the remaining male population. The Queens slither amongst their subjects, and the hush which is heard is their lover's life being sucked from them. There can be no mention of the Queen's past. No talk concerning any wrong they might have done. Even though they were likely the cause of the situation. They ruled, using exposed secrets, when hearing the family talk of grandma, one expects a saint.

The family has trapped itself in a discipline of deception. None of her children would awaken from their allusion. The Queen was portrayed to be a frail old lady. She did plenty to let you know of her past. That woman would cause you to question their created images. Let her pass a sentence on you. There was no escaping. There was no need to confuse yourself using logic. Whatever she imagined became a reality whenever she repeated it. Let one of her images encapsulate you, and you were transformed into meat awaiting the slaughterhouse's hook. There is no way to reason through it. She must be innocent; therefore, you are guilty. One of her princesses looked like an old, worn-out drag Queen after a mugging. One went to collect whatever the other didn't have time to steal.

Let the household them for a week. It will alter their views. Let them know there is no need to confuse issues with facts. The house judges itself innocent. Let them struggle between the rotating rules. Let them know what it is like to embrace hopelessness. To see no reason can reach through its imagination. Let them discover no one questions or volunteers to suffer the Queen's wrath. Let them feel their life fading amid the Queen and her court. Let them endure so the Queen and her court can exist. Introduce them to the house, where truth is sacrificed to secure the Queen's continued performance. Let them endure the acts of her mounting her thrown, knowing she had been inaugurated for it through lies. Let them witness how ill and pail she can become. Let them discover how a few pats of powder can leave a sickly hue to hide her mischievous glow. Let them hear the tormented screams hidden within the laughter. Let them feast on peasant crumbs amongst shelves lined with food purchased with your blood yet belonging to others. Let them watch as her creatures come to devour or destroy your nourishment. Let them know the hopelessness of those who claim they want to know, thinking they can learn through mere words and observations. Let them dread the echo of humanity. Let them fear; "those who do endure do not survive; they absorb until they have become what they feared." Let them search themselves, fearing the monster yet lives in them. Let them struggle to find the strength and the victory of discovering the hollowness of the saying, "The abuse dies with me." Let them hear the house reek with laughter, knowing those outside it cannot grasp its secrets. They haven't a clue about her underground city. They have never met the officer who desires you to purchase from his much-needed supply. They do not see how the authorities are trained to turn their eyes. They know not the horror of the house. They do not understand that our perception of truth can be more binding than truth. If knowledge is based upon experiences, what is the proper way of explaining how it was experienced, and who should decide how it should be communicated? If the abused were to speak another language, I venture to say the language would be studied. However, the abused often misuse the rules of English while talking through their lack of proper diction. We assume the others who have never experienced the abuse still understand how to fill in the missing parts. We are continually commanded to express ourselves in an approved manner or to accept our continuing to be ignored. To express ourselves in such a manner would cost our hopes of obtaining life.

Forgive me for holding onto my hopeless situations. Mere words are hollow. Yet, they are all there is to cling to. It appears so easy to claim that if I were... I should be able to explain. However, knowing and explaining are not interchangeable. Describe for the blind person the warmth in red and the coolness in pastels. Explain to them the energy in abstract art. Tell the deaf of the piano inside the brook of the alarm in escalating syncopation. Describe, for cancer-ridden, the taste of food. Many things are known that words will never contain. Words are a miserable means of communication, yet they are what I have.

The house stood erect. Its lawns were plush in their display of luscious grass. Fresh snow was quickly removed from the walks. and her trees and bushes were manicured. Her windows were clear, though all curtains were pulled shut. She received two fresh coats of white paint every fourth year to remove any effect from natural decay and the changing seasons. I recall my uncle's echo, "Those who do not know their history are destined to repeat it." "Some folks think Lincoln ended slavery because it was the right thing to do. "Others," my uncle claimed," believe that his freeing the slaves was a byproduct of his new party's desire." I've read that some thought the War Between the States was not fought over slavery but over different philosophies. One group believed states should be able to establish their own laws. At the same time, the other felt the federal government should obtain complete control. One group of states called it the Civil War. They believed that the states didn't have the authority to succeed from the union and that their action to dismiss their secession was proper. It's hard to imagine someone having been in a in battle believing War could be civil. The truth regarding the War lies on forgotten battles fields with unrecorded details passed over by those dictating history. Through it all, neither side desired to allow all individuals to have the rights that once were proclaimed self-evident. Taking these rights was done while they claimed we could not grasp the importance of such responsibility. When wars are won, the victor writes the history.

Mr. Lincoln declared a woman, a writer no less, brought about his civil War, as though the wrongs of society had nothing to do with it. The lady simply gave a name to the injustice. The monsters of injustices thrives when a community remains silent, only daring to whisper behind its closed doors. These are twin paths to a painful lesson; silence and rebellion are methods of surrender.

Because the mainstream accepted greenbacks as gold, Mr. Lincoln could finance his War on the allusion to the created money. When he desired more financing, all he needed to do was have it printed and pay the extortionist. Control of the nation's capital was to be under congress. Still, a mere twenty-four percent for the turning of their heads was what the creators of this imaginary wealth considered reasonable. What could it hurt?

The greenback's only value would be what people were willing to place on them, and therein lies the fly of the ointment. Greenbacks' only value is a perceived value. The gold which backed the greenbacks had vanished into the wind. It was perceived that they should borrow upon the belief the nation would improve. It needed to be discovered how the perceived wealth would create perceived power.

Greenbacks became the excepted standard of the bartered system, and the nation believed the north won the War. Whenever more capital was needed, more greenbacks were printed. Those who controlled its printing controlled the wealth of the country. He was killed when Mr. Lincoln thought he no longer needed his creation. The newly excepted system yielded newly formed power to a few elitists. Mr. Lincoln had created his solution for his civil War but failed to grasp the impact of that solution. Though the nation eventually returned to the gold standard, that standard would not be permitted to remain. History records that some desire to rule while others surrender.

Isn't it fascinating that the traits which the elite of society promote are the traits used to manipulate the masses? The world is full of people awaiting their dreams. Watching for "the day" as another passes. Meanwhile, the self-appointed leaders of the day strum the strings, never telling how the last public letters written from the pin of the man who printed, "We hold these truths to be self-evident," contains an alarming confession,

"The general spread of the light of science has already laid open to every view the palpable truth, that the mass of mankind has not been born with saddles on their backs, nor a favored few booted and spurred, ready to ride them legitimately, by the grace of God. (T. Jefferson June 24, 1862.)

The radical protestors of our past have become the politicians of today. They grabbed control when others yielded their dreams. Were they correct, or were they well paid? They cried and demanded change in the streets they'd set aflame, yet they have now settled for an exchange of positions.

I understand most towns have hushed conversations, but the death of Camelot has tried to silence a nation. A surprised world looked on as Camelot bowed her head in sorrow. I understand the town our house chose was not, is not, and shall never be the only town with hidden passages. Nevertheless, that town holds secrets to silence the mass's cries.

When someone is raised amid injustice, they tend to accept whatever is as all there is. I thought the house was unique. We all knew it held evil, but the place was, and that was all we knew. I did not try to find justice. Justice came with the Easter Bunny, Santa, and the other lies people tell children to amuse themselves. Justice is pie in the sky that someone placed in a book to scream to the downtrodden they were once robbed of innocence.

The house sometimes responded differently. Before I went to Kindergarten, I had a good existence.

I could do what I needed, and grandma would not allow anyone to spank me.

Grandma declared, "If he is smart enough to sit on it, they could not pick me up to spank it." What a brat I must have been.

If you desire to destroy a man, do not withhold from him. Give him all he wants. Sit back and watch; he will kill himself. Your quest will be better served in this manner, and the result will be crueler than anything you could have imagined.

When people withhold, the withholding creates a longing. A longing that consumes. The emptiness of that longing could cause one to ask questions, seek, think, and escape. Knowledge, some will tell you, is in the answers. It abides within the questions. How does one appear to be supportive through domination? The answer is misdirection.

Magicians practice misdirection; Politicians practice misdirection, and Comedians, at times, use it.

Misdirection: He wanted to be with her in the worst way.

He was, for richer or poorer. And no hope of a prenuptial now.

Misdirection: I had the meanest dad. One of our neighbors offered to fly us to California. I begged dad. I pleaded with him. Please take him up on his offer and take me to Disney Land. He put that look on his face, pointed to where I was to exit, and barked, "You want to see a rat, move the refrigerator."

Misdirection is only sometimes entertaining.

Have you ever been conversing with someone and noticed their foot pointing in another direction? That is not a conversation; it's misdirection.

Have you ever received a yes from the lips of a head shaking itself no? That is misdirection.

The house often used misdirection to rule. It did not believe in equality or democracy. It held its captives in classes and ruled over the lower class through smoke and mirrors.

Our house could have been divided into two classes: the elite and the impoverished. The elite controlled. They controlled the house, its image, the resources, and the disadvantaged. Their power was not to be challenged. There was the rub. They only ruled as long as the masses did not challenge them. When the mass of humanity speaks, oppressive rulers must take notice or run the risk of discovery.

I know that misdirection was not the only method the house used to conceal all the house had hidden. The house knew each of its victims individually. I am not attempting to tell you how it always happened. I am relating how it sometimes came upon me. If grandma's mind could conceive it. Despite the lunacy of the thought process, if it could be repeated, it became the foundation of the new reality.

Chapter 10

I do not know how or why I fell from grace. I only know I did, which centers on the time right before the divorce. We had rules before mom divorced dad, but new ones came after it. Only some of the regulations before their divorce were bad. Before the divorce, if I got my school jeans dirty twice on the way to school, I was not permitted to go to change them again, which meant no school. Grandma walked into town every Friday. Going to town was an event. Grandma held all money. She purchased things for her subjects. Especially those who lived in the far-off reaches of the perceived queendom.

Most importantly, at lunchtime, grandma went to the diner. They knew her booth. If I happened to be with her, I was rewarded with a cheeseburger, French fries, and coke.

I can't describe what a Friday in school was like during the first grade; however, from a second-grader's perspective, Fridays were the same as Monday through Thursday. At least, they were from my view of a cleared-off corner of the teacher's desk.

It must have been the summer between the third and fourth grades when their divorce came. I could be whooped. Not spanked, WHOOPED. Spankings are mere slaps on the seat of the problem. WHOOPINGS: When one's might is used, you hear the wind swooshing before the thud from the object that has deformed your walking ability for a while. Sitting no longer meant a thing; she began swinging to do damage. I had no need to understand what I did wrong. I was vulgar and destined to grow up and be just like my father. I became the scapegoat for all the evil others had performed against her.

The relationships changed, but at the time, I could not understand why. I only knew I was no longer their little man. I was destined to grow up and become one of "them." If I tried to explain my perspective, I was hit repeatedly. This happened as she commanded the jurors, "Look at the bull. Look at the snot fly." Those about were instructed not to worry because I would never amount to anything.

The princess of the Queen's court had it made. (The Queen is my grandmother after I came of age to be abused. The lesser queens are her favored daughters and granddaughters.) All they needed to do was twist something and run in to tell her whatever they wanted to claim I did. It did not matter how ridiculous it was. Lies became a reality whenever repeated, especially if tears were added. I often thought it would have been easier if I had done the crime. I was a homeless child who knew where his house was. I had a dad; I was never permitted to know. I was a child, alone in a world no one could view.

In the fourth grade, I made a friend. It was with a kid who went to an exclusive private school. He was riding his unicycle past the house. I saw him a few days prior. We went to his house and played when his mom drove up in a nice new car. She didn't even get out of that German beauty before telling me to leave and that she never wanted me to return. Before I was out of range, I heard her explain to her son that my dad was the town's drunk; therefore, I was not to come around. I was kicked out because of a man I was never permitted to know drank. For the longest time, I thought she should have made something up against me. I was also surprised to learn how easily some people can reduce a person to a position of non-importance.

I tried to do right. I tried to do the right things so the queens would once again pretend to like me. The more I tried, the more trouble I got into. The more I tried to be who they wanted, the more the person inside me died.

Chapter 11

Whenever a minor queen came over, and I was there, it meant trouble. Sometimes, I had to go to her house. Sometimes, there were other peons, and we would be taken to her place to be locked out or sentenced to the garage. I always wondered why I had to go. Sometimes, when we arrived, we were given tasks others had determined to be beneath them. Still, doing things went by faster than when I was just locked out for the day.

This is why I became knowledgeable about the river. I taught myself how to fish with the aid of strangers who had befriended me. I knew where to fish based on the catch I was after. Catfish lived on the bottom near underwater cliffs and drop-offs. They liked the places where the rotted liver would drift naturally. The bass lived in the currents or would hide in small pools of calm water behind rocks in the streams. They also stayed near trees or their stumps at the river's edge. Bass liked night crawlers taken from the golf course after the sun went down or soft craws from the water's edge early in the morning. The Queen loved fresh fish. She may have relished in the knowledge she would not have to waste any of our money for our nourishment. Fish, to me, was like people who ask too many questions. After being exposed, they begin to stink.

Once our freezer was fish-filled, I would be told not to bring any more back until requested. All the while, I would trade some fresh fish for a good meal. It was not hard to find grateful people willing to overlook my numerous faults while walking through a depressed community with a nice stringer of fresh fish. Discovering this helped me to hone my skill of misdirection. It is incredible what you can say to hungry people while holding a stringer of fish, providing you smile. It doesn't have to be a natural smile when the fish are large and plentiful. I don't think they listened; they heard words while imagining what they were going to do with those fish.

Watch the way people stand. Their bodies tell a lot. Ask your questions, but watch them answer. Most people always need help to learn the different ways people respond. For example, the man with a digital watch gives the exact time while the man reading the face of one looks and then rounds time off to the nearest quarter hour. These things say something about the people.

I had been taught the art of not giving proper answers. So, I could withstand the questioning and be able to misdirect those pencil pushers who only asked open-ended questions. Questions that were leading, which everyone knew, needed a correct answer. Such training permitted the Queen and her court to leave when desired. They knew we peons were dangling from frayed strings. It was quite a system. We appeared to be answering the questions, and the Queen was permitted to fill in the details we forgot. They could add anything they desired as long as they did so with a smile. Anyone in the Queen's court was permitted to speak. Their purpose of existence was to correct peons.

I was continuously being trained on my part by acts of humiliation or undue punishment. If a wrong answer was given, then all that was needed was for it to be corrected or denied by a few lesser queens. Most times, these acts were performed for the Queen's amusement. The act of separating me from others during their questioning had no effect. I had been schooled in how inapt the system's people were. Furthermore, I believed I did not want to be rescued. It is useless to portray it as the sweet life with all those sour faces looking out the windows of the children's home.

Those in the controlling system proclaimed they did what was best for everyone. Still, boys' bikes were produced with those painful top bars. These strangers said they were knowledgeable, yet they passed laws that forced the builders of banks to put braille keypads on their establishments. How many blind people did these scholars perceive driving to the windows to conduct business?

With the simple use of a question, one could obtain the means to humiliate another regardless of their answer. Was a well-honed form the Queen, and her court had perfected.

"Have you stopped wetting your bed?" To answer in any way was to dawn shame.

These people did not fear the authorities, for those in authority knew nothing. Their humiliation and punishments desired effect was to silence. I was forced to learn the art of internalizing pain.

My brother left the house before he was sixteen.

Dorothy wanted somewhere over the rainbow.

Bobby Bare wanted to go home.

The Beatles wanted some girl's hand.

The Rolling Stones wanted satisfaction.

My brother wanted out.

That escape hatch closed and was guarded behind him, not desiring to lose more victims. I heard plenty of rumors about his going. Still, those who did the talking were never males who turned eight in our house. I learned the necessity of being alone in crowds. The outcasts of the town knew me by name. We survived on our nothingness together. At eight years old, the streets does not pretend to be home. The world quickly points out there is no place to lay your head.

Still, there were good things that occurred. The factory where mom worked had a softball team that practiced near the house. I was a child and did not know the world's workings. I often went to watch her factory's team practice. The players and I became friends. The first basemen and I exceptionally so. He was a massive man with little tuffs of gray starting to peek out around his ears when he wore his cap, but he could clean the bases with one swing of his bat.

I was a runt with long white hair going everywhere. One day, I started getting their bats. It did not go well when some in the town saw me. When it became evident that these men were going to take the towns league trophy home and win the opportunity to play the Reds. The league rulers changed the rules and made them take on some white guy. He only came to a few practices. Still, I did not care when he left. Our shortstop was smoother. That guy slid into second with his nails up during practice, cutting our second baseman from his knee to his growing. One of the guys had a new red Galaxy 500 convertible. He played in the outfield. He bought that car with the money they gave him for going to war in that war, which the news called a police action.

When he came to try out for the team, he took the center field then accepted his job at the factory. He was different but fit in well. When the other players exercised and stretched before practices, he didn't; he went to centerfield and practiced Karate. The team was taking our injured man to the hospital way out of town. He was bleeding all over the exterior of the new Galaxy. I told them to let me show them where a closer hospital was that I went to. Turned out they knew all about the place I went to. I don't think they believed me. Still, some young, prominent city doctor came out into the hall and sewed our second baseman's leg up.

However, other doctors tried to convince us to take him to that other hospital. As I said, the man who owned the factory paid his bills.

Another mistake the cheating guy made as he sat next to me and told me what he would do to my mom. At the house, a saying goes, "Don't sleep, fool." When this jerk came for his bat, I gave it to him. I landed a blow right to his knees. Those men on the team sprinted in. One of them took the bat from me. I was swinging for the fence. They let me kick him for a little while. Before the first basemen carted me off in one of his arms. I heard our center fielder explain it to the guy. "It isn't about black or white. You don't talk about a poor boy's mamma."

I don't recall ever seeing the guy again. There was talk he was looking for me. I also heard the center fielder convinced him otherwise. He said his team's motto in Viet Nam was to liberate the oppressed.

Still, I saw plenty in our closed-eyed, look-the-other-way community. I saw a cross burning in the front yard of a house outside town by the junkyard where dad and I used to visit. It was way out past the fairgrounds. A woman lived there who would talk to anyone. She lived out by our covered bridge. Some walking sheets grabbed her by her hair and pulled her off the porch while others kicked her. They did this to a girl! She covered her head with her hands and tried curling up in a ball. She was crying and screaming. No one came to her aid, even though I am sure many heard. It wasn't dark, and men were in the junkyard. Cars drove past as they kicked her and yelled things at her until two of them began to hold her up. They held her while others urinated on her. Then they grabbed by her hair and made her view their burning cross. I was told they did it to ensure she understood what would happen if she made them return. I never heard what they said, and she refused to tell. They left before I got to her. She held up her hands and told me she'd be alright. I didn't believe her. She warned that it wasn't safe, that they'd be back. But I helped her the best I could to get into her house. The woman couldn't walk; she crawled and dragged herself to the porch.

I once saw one of the star football players. A guy who made all-state. Pick up a trash can and throw it through the windshield of an El Camino at the high school hangout. This happened a block from the square. It was a Friday night after they won the game. People claimed it was because he did not like the guy the girl in the car was with. The guy with the girl that received the trashcan was shot later that night for being black and dating a white girl. People were mumbling something about the town changing. That is the night rumored to have started our town's riot.

The night of the riot did not change the town's people. They simply choose to display who they are. I saw people hitting others. I heard strange sounds. I was with two friends as we were ducking-and-covering our way across town. We were going to our houses until we came to the top of the Market Street Bridge and saw the riot. Once we saw that, we were just going. People said it was the Black Panthers, the Hells Angels, and the KKK. I don't know who they were. I saw three crosses burning on the centerpiece of our town square where the fountain used to be. We snuck our friend behind us while dashing through the back alleys. I did not see a cop that night. Some people later claimed the cops were on the rooftops. Others claimed they were out of town. I know they were nowhere to be seen, and our city received a new modern square once the turnabout was reopened.

I was ordered not to talk about it. Grandma never wanted those snooping outsiders around disrespecting the house.

Still, the house was becoming more and more impossible. Teachers demanded that I think the way they taught. This was different from the way the house was developing our thinking process.

The minor queens began exercising their rights. The younger and less artistic candidates were being interviewed for a future position on the throne. People across the country were burning books and albums. The boy's hair was growing longer, and the girl's dresses and skirts were getting shorter. Things that always were suddenly were not. Places I could go to were being torn down. Other kids were forced to come to my school. There was a constant rumble in the streets concerning the changing times. I was told I was not old enough to understand. All the while, the questioning strangers pretended they held the answers.

Often, if I was caught alone by the authorities, I was asked questions. Sometimes about the men on the team and other times about what was happening in the house. Those men on the team never did me wrong. I knew the art of answering questions without saying a thing. Seldom were those who asked queries the ones who were willing to help. These questioners usually had an agenda in mind; it was not my survival. The team and I got along fine, and they were more than willing to do our talking between the chalk lines. They took the trophy. We drove it right through the center of town. I have heard that they also beat the Reds, but I was not allowed to go to that game. One of them was asked to go play for them.

Rumor was that the man who controlled industry in our town said he did it because it needed to be done. I believed him. I was his paperboy. I delivered a paper he paid for by the year at the newspaper office. When we took that trophy through town, I sat on the back in the middle of the passenger's front seat. My friend helped me to sit up straight. Everyone could see we had the trophy. People were looking and pointing as I took my second but final ride in the beautiful Galaxy 500. That car was clean as a whistle. It had a nice two-tone interior. The town stopped to notice when we drove through with that trophy.

All this was happening while my brother moved out. I had no one to show me the way. I had no one to explain life's lessons. I had no one to warn me. I had no one to act up to release me from the excessive beatings. Before he turned sixteen, my brother moved out. At twelve years old, I was alone in an overflowing house.

Chapter 12

My brother moved into a rundown; upstairs apartment owned by one of the town's biggest slumlords with a few friends. I would walk over at times to visit. Still, things were not the same. Others in our house didn't know where it was. My brother and his friends would sing and sometimes play new records.

Once, they decided to aluminum foil their living room. It took a lot more than we figured. I went back to the house and cleaned it out of foil. When their living room was finished, it looked cool, but it was hot. It didn't take long to start pulling the foil down.

Once, I was there, hanging out, when someone passed me a joint. I do not know where my brother came from, but as the joint came to me and I started to raise it, my brother tapped me on the shoulder and nodded for me to follow. We stepped into the kitchen, where he told me, "That is not the way. There are places it will take you which no one needs to go. If I catch you doing it, I will stomp you."

My brother's room had been the attic room when he lived with us. He and his friends would listen to music there. They also practiced and recorded their music. He was quickly found when he came around. He sang songs by Taylor, Guthrie, King, Young, John, and Dylan. CCR, the Dead, and the one by the Animals. I sang along with him to the song about the house. He played his guitar upside down because he was left-handed. Shortly before his graduation, he was killed in a car crash. The coroner claimed he hadn't suffered. I couldn't help but shake my head at that statement.

When his funeral precession passed the high school to the graveyard, the seniors lined the high school's lower-level windows. I was told there were no classes that day because the school just talked about it and played tapes of him singing. There were two others from his class that were with him. His oldest and best friend lived. However, he was seriously hurt and still in the hospital during my brother's funeral. During the graduating precession, they left open spaces as if all three were making the journey with them. While alive, he was never accepted at the school, but somehow death changes people's perspective.

During that period, we used to wear English riding boots. The style was to extend the boots' life by adding horseshoes. Mom gave a hundred dollars for them, but they lasted three times longer than the sixty-five-dollar penny loafers we used to wear. The schools in town decided they would not tolerate people they called hippies, so they decided we could no longer wear boots with horseshoes. On the same day, my brother and I were kicked out of two different schools for violating a dress code that never existed. They called mom in from the factory. She first came by to pick me up from junior high, but only because I was the closest. She pulled into the football stadium's parking lot and parked. Then, I was demanded to stay.

Like I was some dog. She walked across the street and up the steps to the high school. She walked into the front of the building. She returned without him, but her steps had quickened, and the principal was coming after her, threatening something. Finally, mom turned and screamed, "Do it, just kick him out and see what that gets you." I later learned from my brother that one of the teacher's kids walked by the office where he was being held. The guy had long hair, was wearing faded elephant bells, and had on boots like ours. Mom asked who he was and why he wasn't being suspended. Through the years, wondered why she bothered asking. Mom knew it was because of who we were that our treatment was different. My brother told me how mom got up in the face of the principal. She told him she was a single mother with one kid in college, three teenage boys at home, and a child in elementary school. She explained that she worked like a dog to keep clothes on our backs, food in our bellies, and a roof over our heads. She told him the boots were staying unless he wanted to pay for our shoes. She got in the car and told me to get ready. She kicked me out at the junior high school, where I was gladly welcomed. Our schools never cared much for my brother. They were constantly kicking him out and calling mom about something he'd done. Strange how those same people talked differently about him once he died.

Once, my brother came back to the house saying he'd been shot. Mom was carrying on as she took him to the hospital. She said someone threw a firecracker that managed to get inside his boot. She said it blew away a chunk of his calf when it went off. They never figured out who did it, though she would state it must have been some other troubled youth. Everyone knew the children in other parts of town were not permitted to perform mischief. I have my own opinion of the incident. I know messing with black powder can get touching at times.

My brother was the first of her kids to be arrested. He spent three days in the county jail. He was dating a police chief's daughter, although he was the chief in a nearby town. The cops found my brother, his best friend, and their girls under blankets, on the levy near the old, covered bridge. His best friend was from a well-off family, but his girl was only the fire chief's daughter. Anyway, the cops jerked off my brother's blanket. There they were, him and his girl in all their glory. The Queen and her court lived that up. Until mom spoke, and it had to be squelched. No one else from the event was taken in, and he went to jail. None of the others were charged with a thing. They tried to get him for indecent exposure but couldn't because they had removed his blanket. They said they were holding him for contributing to the delinquency of a minor as a minor.

Mom was crying the day the DA came to get his laundry. He was a good man. He never once talked down at us. He would squat down and look at me when he talked. I heard him ask mom why she was crying, but he asked out of concern. When he discovered her teenage son was locked up in the adult jail (I spilled the beans), he volunteered to represent him. When mom explained what she knew to him, he discovered my seventeen-year-old brother was being detained without her being notified. That the only way we found out was by one of his friends coming by to tell. The DA became a man on a mission. My brother was released in no time. The case never went to trial. All his charges were instantly dropped, and we had ourselves a lawyer.

One time one of my brother's girls needed a place to stay. He assured her she could bunk with us. I can't believe what he said while trying to convince mom to let her sleep in our room. He was younger when he tried to pull that one off. It never happened. At least, that's how mom tells it.

The ordinary people in town said our DA was "quite a man" because when the powers had instructed him to do something he found immoral, he refused. It was rumored he had warned them he'd quit first. Those people in town were glad when he did. He never looked back. He was known in the city as the man who tried to explain that just because something is legal doesn't mean it is correct. The man got me off once.

Two wealthy children, two poor kids, and I were playing in an oak tree at the baseball field across from the poor kid's elementary school. Some cops driving by spotted us. The other poor guys got away. The rich kids' lack of escaping knowledge caused me to be captured. I still don't know what we did wrong because kids always climbed those old oaks. Anyway, this day, I was grabbed and put in the back of a cop cruiser. One of the cops read something to me and asked if I understood. I knew before they read it to me, I was not talking. One of the cops shut the door and was getting in, so I could be in transport. Out of nowhere, my lawyer showed up. I later discovered he lived at the edge of the ball field and came over to see what was going on close-up. They let him talk with me. We were somewhat left alone after he told them he would represent me. Apparently, he had been watching. He asked the cops why the other children weren't being charged or asked to leave the tree. The cops were shocked. They had not noticed the wealthy children. The three of them walked under and then looked into the tree. My lawyer was smiling as they discovered who they were. Then softly, slowly, but firmly, he explained to them. They needed to arrest those two who were the children of the who's who of our town, or they could release me.

I was never in jail, except once; even then, I went to help the cops. One day, my friend and I were walking around uptown when a cop came out of their station and yelled at us. We were off in a flash. We ran into the dime store and hid between old ladies' dresses in their racks. I was worried I would get booked for resisting an arrest. My brother had a friend who drove his old army jeep on the levy and was arrested for resisting an arrest. When he stood before the judge, they only got him for resisting an arrest. Before then, I had no idea you could resist an arrest that hadn't occurred. I decided I would go back and turn myself in and face whatever charges they had against me. One should never assume a good lawyer can get them off. In my hometown, people said they could arrest anyone they wanted. I knew the laws were different in town. One of the wealthiest women in town took things from stores. The police said arresting her wouldn't be proper. She was a victim of some awful phobia. The local stores and shop owners followed or had someone follow her around their places to write down what she'd taken. They then sent the bill to her accountant, who'd promptly pay. She came by our house with not much more than a rag once. She wanted mom to use that thing as a pattern and then sew it back together. This woman painted her apartments in mink stoles. She constantly drove about in brand-new Cadillacs and used them like work trucks. She never knew a stop sign was for her, but let some fool hit her and find out who was at fault. It was said she knew the town's gigolos by their names. In my hometown, wealthy folks were diseased. It was the poor who were your typical common criminals.

I'd considered who I was, persuaded myself to return, and turned myself in. The police station had just received new TV cameras. The cops wanted us to try to hide from them so they could see if they could detect us on their monitors. After a while, I excused myself and went back for my friend. He was still in those old ladies' dresses. It was amazing the kids you could meet in those spaces between the racks of the old ladies' dresses. I explained to him what they wanted from us. We had to tell some of the other kids they couldn't come. We had a blast that day, but the cell doors were never closed, and they fed us.

Chapter 13

My oldest sister had the highest grade point average in her high school graduating class. Still, she wasn't permitted to be the valedictorian because those honors couldn't be awarded to a girl. Not to mention, she was one of us, or she was in their eyes. Someone whose family had supported the proper politician fathered the young man they recognized as the valedictorian. He only scored the third highest. Another girl scored better than he did as well.

One of the wealthy and well-known people in our town found out my sister did not receive her scholarship. It really upset the lady. She called mom to ask some questions, to which I believe she already knew the answers. She told mom to pick up my sister and come into town to meet with her at her clothing store. These stores were little mom-and-pop shops to the casual observers. Still, they were the pilot stores owned by people who owned what would become substantial chain stores across our nation. These owners were called "old money. "Old money did not come to our part of town to help. They sometimes came to buy houses or people, but they did not come to help. Anyway, she told mom that she did not believe it was right. Her scholarship money was stipulated for the person who scored the highest grade point average. My sister never missed a math or science problem throughout high school. You have to decide if you want to believe that because I heard about it often enough to know it may not be valid. The shop owner helped mom by matching the valedictorian's scholarship. My sister was her graduating class valedictorian of college.

While she went to college, she worked across the road from the YWCA, where she stayed. It was some little dinner that allowed her to have flexible hours and a little spending cash. Also, there was a rumor that the old money lady started giving her old money to those who earned her scholarship directly. She no longer trusted the system to announce the winners at graduation. There is more to this than rumored because the old money ladies in town started talking amongst themselves. These wives outlived their husbands for the most part. Those old money ladies did not like what was happening, and since everything else in the world was upside down, they figured they might as well set some things right. All this may seem like it does not matter, but it proved change was possible. I learned from those ladies that rulers take notice when the masses come together.

Chapter 14

Once, I was sent out in the hall because I proved the earth was round and orbiting the sun. It was in ninth-grade earth science. Later, I was expelled from school by that teacher for thinking. I wish I had that slip. He expelled my brother, too, and I had been warned to watch out for me. They said he did not like long hair and was untouchable because he was the department head. His tenured soul was my first classroom teacher. He was the first teacher of my ninth-grade year, which was my first year of High School. My first class in the school my brother was attending when he died. When that school year started, the man who tried to kick out my brother for having long hair, faded Levi's, and boots asked the entire school to bow their heads for a silent moment of prayer. That silence was interrupted by my voice exploding: "You hated his guts while he was alive, don't kiss his ass now he's dead." It was more than I could take. It was my first day in that school, the first thing in the morning and without any warning... hypocrisy.

When I could go back to school, I was greeted by the earth science teacher again. The man called me by my dead brother's name. I removed myself from his assigned seating and headed back to the office. Even today, it's odd to think about how death makes saints out of sinners in some perverted minds.

"Oh, Jackson, you mustn't talk of people like that." I've been instructed once the person is dead. Death doesn't change the facts; say what you must, just tell the truth. I don't know of a single incident where a dead person came back to retaliate against someone who has done so.

Again, for the next few days, fishing was okay. I had gone to that school twice and was awarded a special guidance counsel. I was introduced to him on my return. An ex-marine who never had anyone under their junior year before me, and then he could only be assigned 10 problem male students. I achieved this in two weeks but less than an hour on the two days I had attended into my freshman year. The world was upside down. It was nice to know some people sometimes did the right things just because they were the right things to do.

My oldest brother was born with special needs but never suffered from retardation. He enjoyed it. He was as ignorant as others needed him to be. I have heard him brag to strangers that he did not need a fishing license because of his condition. I understand that the politically correct way of explaining this would have been to say he was challenged. Still, that would disrespect my brother and all he'd been through. He is the oldest son, but he still picked dandelions from the fields for mom until she passed. He was still asking mom when our brother was coming back; he was in his early seventies when she died. When he was a kid, he was big, not fat; he was big. He had the figure of an inverted Christmas tree.

As a boy, he could have hunted bears with popsicle sticks and returned with a kill.

Before I was born, the man who controlled industry in our town came to talk with mom. He sat at our table and drank the coffee. He then explained he wanted to pay for my brother's special education. Though the system had failed, he didn't. It is nice to know some people do the right thing because it is correct.

That same man gave mom a job cleaning his and some of his other mansions, including the one downtown, which his company's bigwigs used to stay in when they came to visit to learn from him. He later hired her as the first female non-clerical employee in his factories. The man had quality control before the rest of the industries knew what it was. He led the industry. He did not believe in waiting for the industry to guide him.

He bought a computer that took up the second floor of one of his facilities, which took up two entire city blocks. Still, if you were to have met him, you'd never know he had two nickels. He was the definition of old money and had more than anyone around. Still, he did not play the role. The man who controlled industry in our town was as common as dirt. He gave orders to the well to do the up-and-comers and bent down so we could look each other in the eyes when conversing with me. He would get down on his knee, but his wife snubbed me like the others who had to play their parts. Still, he remained loyal to the people.

His wife was taken about in her servant-driven limo. The servant had to stare off into space while opening her car door. He wore white gloves so he would not tarnish its chrome or highly polished finish. Yet her husband, who remanded the source of her opulent lifestyle, drove about town in an old car that Ford once gave him. Our town was blessed by his giving, both privately and publicly. The man never looked down on anyone that I know of. He'd shake my hand and thank me for the excellent way I launched his paper onto his vestibule when I came by weekly to collect my tip. I used to laugh because I knew the maid delivered his newspaper when she delivered his breakfast. That man did not venture out his door to get the paper; his wife would not dream of allowing that. He wouldn't have minded, except it would have cost his maid her job.

Once, a tiny child was out near the duck pond he had built for his wife to gaze upon. It was a miniature replica of the one in Washington seen on postcards. They had to create a pumping station at the bottom of the hill to get water up to the pond to keep it from stagnating, so I was told. It was a bricked-style pump house trying to be disguised as a millhouse. The millhouse with a water wheel that never spun and popped up at the bottom of the hill, which still had a higher elevation than most of the town. A mill house there to pump water up Snob Hill, miles from any natural water source.

We played hide-n-seek in the tunnels behind the planks used in the pond's dam and ran to the fake millhouse. Once, a child turned a big wheel or something at the tunnel's opening. This thing opened, and it somehow drained the pond a little, but it flooded the homes at the bottom of the hill on the far side of the street. Those children thought it was great that their part of town finally was flooded, and they went john-boating down the road until the problem was corrected.

Anyone who truly had arrived lived on the hill. Their last name may have been spelled differently, but those on Snob Hill, by need, blood, or marriage, were part of the right family.

One day, a child from the hill fell into that pond. A man heard him splashing, crying, and screaming for help. The man ran to save him. He was hired as Snob Hill's groundskeeper. Folks never questioned why he was there. Not even by those permitted to live on Snob Hill. When he heard the screams, that man jumped fences to save the little boy. He was not comfortable speaking because of his stammering. I was told it was part of his war injuries. People talked about his salary throughout our town. The rumor was he made an x on his checks. He told me he was in the woods hunting mushrooms that day; he taught me how to pick them.

When I delivered the morning paper, he would be in the orchard tending to his business when I came through. The mist in the form of steam would rise off the lawns. He'd be up on a long-tapered ladder in one of the trees tending to its needs. I sometimes waved, and he'd often motion me over to toss my breakfast when the fruits were ripe. He lived in a little house built on Snob Hill for him. The man was even paid to maintain his own place. Gentle old soul. Reluctantly, he spoke to people. He would converse with the employer. I talked with him. Pretending I did not notice his trouble speaking helped.

Still, mostly, he would motion what he wanted me to do. Once, he needed to figure out what to do after I found what I thought to be an artisan well. It was just a leak in the sprinkler system. A sprinkler in my town was decadent. If you didn't like the weather, give it a half hour, and nature would come up with one to your liking. I considered him my friend. He knew about the lawns and how to fry catfish. I called him Harvey after Jimmy Steward's friend. I never knew his given name. Things you could hear about him in town would fill a book. Most people had plenty of titles to belittle him, but they never bothered conversing with him; they only talked at him or about him. It was like he grew invisible. He was a quiet old soul, content with himself and his remaining life.

Harvey told the man who owned the property on the top of the hill and controlled industry that I found the break in his watering system. WHAT A TIP! A brand new stiff one-hundred-dollar bill. Mom said I couldn't keep it. I did. Grandma told me to give it to her to hold. I told her I had lost it. That money bought potato chips, sodas, and models of funny cars, including the glue and paints needed to assemble them correctly for a few friends and me. My brother borrowed a few bucks so he could get some stuff.

Chapter 15

When I went to school, if the teacher knew my oldest sister, they called on me to answer the tough questions. If they knew my oldest brother, they wanted me to carry things, and if they knew my brother who died, they wanted me to sing their favorite song. To make matters worse, I had cousins who had attended this school. This only added to their confusion.

When I participated in school, few in the school's system allowed me the freedom to be who I was. I was a kid who questioned people who claimed they held answers to the world upside down. It seemed incredible how they could not grasp that content people were those who had grown to be comfortable with themselves.

As societies grew older, there were those in positions to glean from their corruption. Every great civilization developed people who desired to rule the world. History records a few have gotten close, though they have yet to accomplish that feat. Societies need a social cleansing to rid themselves of the pollutants of such rulers.

When I was a kid, we were amid such a cleansing. The people of the corrupt system seemed to say they knew the way but were stumbling in the same rut as past generations had.

The big stores downtown were the usual ones for the era. Firestone, JC Penny's, and Montgomery

Wards. Most of our stores looked like small mom-and-pop shops.

When I was a little kid, the town was alive. One summer day, for Christmas, Grandma took me to Firestone so I could get my first new bike. I wasn't allowed to tell anyone. She said she'd take it back. With help from grandma, I picked out a powder blue one with a banana seat and ape hangers. The bike was hidden from the others in my oldest sister's closet for months. When Christmas came, we all received new bikes. My brother's new bike was a stingray; it was golden. That bike had hand breaks and a three-speed shifter. It was the one I first asked for, but I was told it needed to be a better-quality bike.

Montgomery Wards was located across from the central police station, which we called the cop shop. One day, when we walked to town, it was gone. Not the building, the store, and all the merchandise in it was gone. The signs in the display windows announced it had closed. This was before Firestone believed in radials. Firestone was the tire to beat when I was young. It was before the downtown suffered because chain stores funneled the town's money back into their communities. Before, people drove to fast-food restaurants to pick up what they called hamburgers.

It was strange; our Montgomery Wards just picked up and left. I asked why. I liked Montgomery Wards. The people there knew me by name. They had a grumpy old man who ran their Otis Elevator. "Why! Before Otis, elevators were an adventure. To get in an elevator before Otis was risky." He was proud to claim. The man would not put up the gate until everyone stepped back from the yellow line on the floor, and he declared the two floors were level. Some people wouldn't take his elevator because they'd rather complain about him being trash. I liked to tell him the baby screaming was my sibling and was scared and upstairs by herself whenever I heard a baby cry. He was a good old man but easily flustered. Because of that old grump, I liked Montgomery Wards.

The reason they closed was they had been robbed. Their entire store was carried off in a single night. The corporate office refused to restock. They said they would relocate into one of the malls beginning to appear. They kind of did, but Wards was never the same as Montgomery Wards.

Many claimed Montgomery Wards was never the same after FDR ordered the secretary of war to seize properties belonging to Montgomery Wards. Montgomery Wards did not comply with his labor agreement. Now they were choosing, and it would to being called Wards cost them their hometown, downtown, feel. They didn't keep the grumpy old men. When I was a kid, old people were meaner, but they knew their business. Those new employees Wards hired didn't know a thing but how to push a sale. The most significant problem downtown businesses faced when they moved to the malls was the competition next door. It made comparing prices easier, and it took much longer to go shopping. Wards never felt the same as Montgomery Wards. As a society, we devoured our downtowns, believing we were saving a buck. But in fact, we weakened our communities by accepting the illusion of lower-priced big box stores.

I was out fishing soon after the robbery when this down and outer asked if I knew how a whole store could be carried off in a single night with the cop shop right across the street, and not one of them saw a thing. I asked that same question of the good man who once was our DA when he came to pick up his laundry. I did it just like the down and outer instructed me. The ex-DA got down and studied me, then asked why I asked. I told him about the other man. He told me I might have solved his case and asked to meet with the down and outer. I arranged for it to happen just like I was told. I told him we'd be fishing by the lighthouse, across from the Dairy Queen, up from the boathouse's playground, upriver, and around the bend. Remaining out of sight from ordinary folk, like I was asked to do. I told him we'd be there all day despite the fishing or hour. I told him we'd wait for him so he could come once his day had ended.

When the old DA came to the river, he had on a starched pale blue with a red pin-striped shirt and soft gay pants that were pleated and cuffed at the bottoms so just the tips of his shoes peeked through. His penny loafers were polished better on the riverbank than at the store. I could only view this while he was in stride and walking horizontally to my waiting spot. Anyway, his shoes had hard, slick bottoms that needed to be scuffed to grip tile floors correctly., but he came to the river as himself. His tie was off, and his sports jacket as well, but you could tell he had worn them because of the wrinkle pattern in the shirt. His hair was perfect, with just a hint of gray starting to show. I never saw him in anything that looked worn or had a flaw. I also have never seen him in a suit. There was something about him that made me feel comfortable. I liked that he came to the river as himself. When he came to us, he squatted down, and I could tell his shoes did not even have a scratch, and his socks were coordinated with his shirt. He said, "Hello, Jackson." We exchanged pleasantries then I introduced him to the down and outer. He asked if they might be excused. I was okay with it. Still, I grabbed my pole from the yoke of the stick I propped it in. Gathered some bait and tackle, then headed off to drown some worms.

The rumors started the man had taken a poor guy's case and solved the mysterious downtown robbery. Some rich people became upset. Some thought they had captured another low life, but they had to set him free. Those same people were upset over it, claiming just because he didn't commit that crime shouldn't matter - they knew he was guilty of other crimes. Supposedly, the cops of the night shift pulled off the robbery. It was good to know some people do the right things just because they're right.

Chapter 16

My dad's race toward death quickened after his divorce from Mom. He was in and out of the hospital until his passing. I can't recall a single time he was admitted to one before their divorce, but he regularly went back after it. I used to sneak off to go see him. The people in the hospital said I wasn't old enough to come alone. Mom said she shouldn't go because they were divorced. She also said, "Just because I can't live with him doesn't mean I don't love him."

My sister was working. Her office was right by the VA where he died, but she wouldn't help me unless there was something in it for her. My brother wouldn't have a thing to do with him, plus he moved out. I had to go by myself. I could walk forever then, so the trip into and across town didn't stop me. I was still trying to get to know dad.

Some doctors or nurses would walk past and try to put me out of their hospital. I'd sneak back in. If they wanted to stop me again, I would run downstairs to slide into the space behind the coke machines and kick the hands of anyone trying to move the machines. Sometimes, they would still capture me and carry me out of their hospital. Other times they had to run to the aid of someone. To this day, I believe they should have allowed me to stay. I was not running through their halls. I was not causing anyone trouble. I did not wish to break their rules. I sat quietly with him, trying to get to know my dad.

Most of the time, he could not talk. His body was betraying him. It appeared puffy and was an awful color. If I were to get too close, while his oxygen mask was needed' but not worn, it seemed to take away his breath. Visiting dad was not pleasant. Somehow, I felt it was needful. A man dying in front of you as a kid is alarming. Such deaths are a little harder to deal with when the man dying in front of you is the one who is supposed to live forever. I understand the hospital staff viewed me as a kid in elementary school. I was his kid who happened to be in elementary school.

Occasionally, he was able to recover enough to get out. We would go for a ride once more. I liked going through the country with the top down. Then he would have a relapse and be right back in their hospital each time his stay would be longer. Each time aged him. Each time, various hospital staff members explained to me why they did not want me at their hospital. Each time they'd do the talking and refuse to listen. They said let's talk to begin the scolding, and then they would not listen. They often closed their lecture by stating, "These are the rules, and that is it." They were wrong. That was my dad, and that was it.

All this happened when two of the minor Queen's worlds fell apart. Her two oldest children were taken to the Children's Home. At least some people claimed it to be a children's home; I never knew a kid there calling it that. That same great aunt and uncle who helped my brother and me rescue her oldest daughter. She didn't stay with them long. There were all types of things being loudly whispered about her of the things she did. Things were being said about her mom, her last husband, and even her newest man. That last husband had done some wild things in his past, but they were talking more about something he was doing then.

I don't know all that happened. It wouldn't be right to tell you what happened. All I know is the great aunt and uncle who were there for me. Whenever I needed them showed up when no one else would. No one else in the family would have stepped up for the minor Queen. It was because of something the little Queen did, but I do not know what it was. They would not allow anyone to stay. The most prominent rumor about this happening was that the little Queen had men slipping through her bedroom window at night. When she left them, I can't remember where she went, but this was the first time she got married. They were just kids; no one expected it to last. At least, that is what was said after their divorce. This happened around the time of her mom's third or fourth divorce. (I wonder if she ever married some of her guys.) Anyway, when all this was happening, their family was scattered. I cannot tell you where all the kids went, but rumors were flying. I thought things would get better. I thought two queens had fallen. I was being given an education; queens are not like peasants. Divorces do not weaken queens; they strengthen them. A queen can lie, cheat, and steal, and it is okay for their role to rule and extend the boundaries of the Queendom. Still, during this period, the Queen briefly lost the rule of her subjects.

Therefore, she came to the house to gather its peons to fill that void.

This period ended when a deal was struck. The youngest of the queens, who was now rumored about town to be another troubled youth, would return from obscurity and go to beauty school. She would study hard and become a hairdresser. In return, mom would foot the bills, and the young Queen would come over to wash and comb out grandma's floor-length hair weekly. She finished schooling. Mom paid all the bills, but she did not do grandma's hair except for once.

While she was studying until the wee hours of the night, she discovered another momentary love of her life. She met him when she went uptown to drive her mother home, who was too far gone to walk. He was her mother's man. When this youngest Queen reappeared, she came with her mother's man and was having his baby.

We had to visit them in that tiny upstairs apartment to take them some of their needed things, which were purchased with our monies. We were schooled in doing without so others could have. It was explained to us that they were happy. Still, the young Queen with the child seemed to cry a lot. Her man was much older than her.

Her latest victim thought he had a catch, not knowing he'd been captured. She was going to have a little girl. This was before they looked to tell people what they were really having. When the little Queen had her child, the realm of the Queendom had to take notice. Still, we of the house carried the brunt of this burden; for there were things to be purchased for her magical child at the house's expense.

Food was removed from our mouths so the expecting mother could be given everything she thought a princess might desire; nothing was too good for a queen, her husband, boyfriend, or magical child. I remember shopping for them because I could not stay at the house alone, "It would not look right."

The Queen would go shopping to buy out a store for the others while explaining we would not be receiving Christmas that year due to the cash shortage. Our table's food was given so the Queen and her family could gorge themselves. I can only remember four times from my childhood that I received Christmas presents, though I cannot recall one which the other realms of the Queendom went without. Not getting gifts while knowing the others received plenty was normal. My brother was killed in a car crash 7 days before her boy was born. I was no longer welcome at the house when her baby came to live with mom. They did not come; the baby came for mom and the queens to raise.

Chapter 17

On the day dad passed, we were told we had to go to my sister's company's picnic. It was going to be in some big park in the big city and have free carnival rides; furthermore, I was commanded to have a good time, but I still did not want to go. I sensed that something wasn't right. Finally, I got them to call the VA. Or they claimed to have called and reported that dad was having the best day of his stay. My sister returned from the back of the house upon hearing the phone ringing. Mom went to answer it. I said, Dad's dead." The Queen smacked me on the back of my head, trying to correct me for talking in that manner as if my words could have caused his death. The person on the phone asked to speak with my eldest sister. When she placed the phone to her ear and said, hello, this is... her color changed, her face fell, and as she stood there with the phone staring at me. After a moment or two, she thanked the person who called. She handed mom the phone and informed the others that dad had passed. They all knew she they busted.

My sister called his family. His people treated mom like she was his bride. His brother said dad wanted to be buried out of state in his family's cemetery. His plot is in the rear of the old family plantation. His grave is in line with the entrance and below a cedar he once was said to have admired. Mom and we kids stayed at his brother's place. His family from all over the country visited us and told us to stop by to see them. I said to this one old lady that we did not know who they were, and after that, I was instructed to visit more often. She looked at me and said, "Honey, you just get to town and go to any house with a mailbox with your last name. Knock on that door. Tell them whose boys you are, and we'll come to you." I never lived in Olive Hill and haven't even as much spent a night there, but those words or her smile helped her statement ring true and made me feel accepted. At dad's viewing, people walked in to visit with others, or talk about the all-in-nothing, and eat. Someone started smacking dad's face while telling him to get out of that box. I left the room, trying to get away and make sense of it. In that state, the last two inches of a grave had to be dug within minutes of lowering the casket. I was asked if I would like the honor of digging those inches. I did not know that relatives came to my uncle telling the world how hard the ground was and how they had to blast his grave to make his final home in the slate cover hillside. Again, I left the room to return to those who had come to meet old friends and eat. Decisions were being made, but this time, dad's brother and the others of his family made sure they heard my voice.

I remember I did not want mom to ride in the limo. Dad's brother called me aside to talk with me. When he said the others might need her. I stopped and asked her to ride with us. Mom road that winding uphill path. She stayed at dad's brother's place. They called her by name and treated her better than the house ever had. It must have been hard to have been accepted by the family she divorced herself from.

I was given dad's flag after his services, but I had to walk about and search for the brass after the sailors fired their shots at the nothingness. Someone told me I could not keep the brass. It is with the flag. Some said I was too young to understand just because they could not live together did not mean they did not love each other. Even as a child, I knew the house was a place to survive. It was never a place that would falsely be accused of supporting life.

My brother passed in May; Dad followed in October. Passing one week lacking five months of my brother's passing. I was going on fourteen. My baby sister is five years younger than me.

When my cousin, once removed, was delivered, he came to the house as his mother had, but he was given to mom, not grandma.

Though grandma's past was off limits, it was nonetheless suspected, though wrapped in secrecy. Once, it was told how she was threatened by an abusive new husband as another guy abused her daughters.

She left town when I was little to live with her sister. When she came back, she went to the house. Her daughter, a lesser queen, once told dad, "She ain't your mom." He gave her a look while stating she was the only mom he'd ever known. Dad never liked that lesser queen and did not like her or those she'd drop off at the house. Dad's mother died when he was three from complications extending from his birth. His dad died when he was beginning the third grade. The way dad explained it for the lesser queen real slow helped her understand she needn't try to correct him on the subject again.

During the summer break from school, after my brother's passing, some girls who liked him came to me at the pool and introduced themselves. These girls showed me the ropes of high school.

I knew I could never be my brother. I was just a kid trying to lay low until my brother hit it big. He said he would come back for me.

It all passed when I was almost fourteen.

My name is Jackson. Raised in a land where we hold these truths to be self-evident.

Nurtured under the constant threat of losing them.

I am a member of the most minor family in the Queen's court.

We are the only family to have never had a queen.

I am the lowest member of that family.

Chapter 18

Early morning, my cell rang while I was out back preparing equipment for the day. Someone I had never met desired to talk with me concerning the child trafficking case. She had been contacted by the person from the FBI my oldest sister contacted, and now the state's child's advocate wished to ask me a few questions. She wanted me to tell her what the county records should have documented. First, she wanted to know if I knew the details of past family members' charges, their arrest records, and the past rulings. I told her I would only know what a child would have been permitted to know.

During the conversation, I discovered she represented the children and wanted me to know that the state made it difficult for a minor's records to be opened. I recall wondering if no one was ever permitted to view the cases, as she claimed, why the records were kept. I told her I'd heard a lot. I suspected more but only knew details about the things that affected me. I tried to explain that in a house filled with lies, few facts are ever viewed as known. I told her I did not know all the details concerning the history of those they were questioning. I did, however, tell her where and what records I would have tried to look up if I were in her position. It seemed as though she was asking me to give her answers to how anyone could have done it. It almost seemed as if she were preparing to defend him. I believe they were trying to avoid any surprises if it ever went to trial, which I did not believe it would. I think she was pulling for my sympathy or was trying to convince me she didn't have the time or manpower to look through all those old records. I did not understand why they were lacking or didn't bother looking through the city's old newspaper. If she were not so concerned with what he had done as she was trying to unfold how it could have happened, the answer might have found its way to her. She was grasping for something to explain how anyone could commit such acts and yet be at peace with themselves. She was searching for the logic behind illogical actions. Why would anyone record the raping of an eight-year-old boy?

She never asked, but she wanted to know how the monster had been created.

She wanted to know how the authorities could have been fooled so badly. The man in custody had passed both the police and fire academies.

I asked the lady questioning me if she ever noticed some of the things salespeople convinced the blind to wear.

I had nothing new to tell her, being sure a person in her position had read the story of *The Emperor's New Clothes*.

She asked when the last time I had contact with family members.

She didn't appreciate that I told her to look up the court's files on forgotten family history. She desired to gain some understanding of his presence as though it had not arrived from the past. She wanted to know and yet placed some events outside of her equation. She did so because she did not desire the alarm of someone she had presumed to be innocent in that view.

There is something that most who have known the street observe. Whenever and wherever you find good people, bad people camp nearby. They need to be together to balance the world. Only sometimes one discovers a man with the integrity of the old DA. Few contribute to their community's well-being as the man who once controlled industry. Those in the system believe they have everything under control, although a few minor flaws need to be addressed.

The man who controlled our industry bought the first computer in our area. After doing so, people gathered from all around to see the thing. He allowed his factory to be used to help establish our new standard of record keeping by allowing tours. These tours must have hindered his realization of his company's growth. He went into town. Into the town's central bank, the one right off our square. The bank that everyone in the city seemed to use. The bank school children took a field trip to open their first savings account. He went to this bank and offered to buy them their computer if they agreed to take over the tours. People came from miles around to switch to our transformed bank. This computer allowed the bank to earn extra money by keeping the books and doing the billings for the local utility companies.

When I was a kid, our banks advertised who had robbed them. Banks had bronze or brass plaques embedded into their vestibules, advertising to potential customers who had robbed them. The amount they had gotten away with, and the day the robbery occurred. They had massive fronts with statues hovering over them, looking like they were there to protect the people's money. They had gigantic glass fronts, huge hardwood counters, stacked moldings running through their coffered ceiling, and those plaques. I used to believe they were proud to have been robbed. The plaques did make it appear as though they were bragging. They were admitting to having been robbed, but only by the best. I remember wondering if they thought the plaques made people feel safer about leaving their money.

"We have been robbed, but only by Floyd, Clyde, and Dillinger."

"Here, sir, please take my money. I sure don't want some armature spending it."

As a kid, we had to take a small amount of change to school every Tuesday to get our good citizenship awards. Put it in on Tuesday and take it out come Friday. That was grandma's rule. She would tell me to get my stuff out of it. "Yah can't take it with you. It's for spending."

The new computer was placed in their basement. They had wide, significant, beautiful marble steps going down to a little landing. The landing was divided in half by brass-plated jail house bars with a barred door. Most people on the street thought the special accommodations in the computer room were for those snooty programmers. Computers ran hot. Their byproduct (heat) destroyed them. They used to keep computers near HVAC units to help cool them. For security purposes, its closeness to the HVAC and the ease of dividing the computer personnel from the regular banking staff made the basement the most economical choice. Still, it was not appreciated by the townspeople who took the tour to see the contraption.

The Lady from the FBI wanted to know who was who in our family. Also, she wished to know how we all were related. They were more than just a little confused by the members who used multiple names. The woman asked if I was shocked when I heard this type of thing had happened.

I recalled the basic information given in the second law of thermodynamics, "things left to themselves deteriorate." Because of this rudimentary understanding, I could not tell her I was shocked. In fact, I had predicted they would have trouble with him before I escaped.

Basically, I felt he didn't have a chance.

This woman wanted me to forget my life's experiences, my parental teaching, the royal substitutes teaching, and all my public school's playground education and talk to her, a stranger.

Some government officials believe that once they identify themselves, we no longer consider them strangers.

"You work for the government. Why I believe you must be trustworthy. Get over here and let me spill my guts."

At one time, I thought I knew things; I was too afraid to talk about them. I understood no one would come to my aid. I once saw things that were not right. I once could see things others thought they had covered up. Then, I was left to ponder and look in the direction of my thoughts.

If the truth sets one free, what did the lies do?

The belief remained. Most people did not care to understand. They liked living in worlds of smoke and mirrors. I suspect most appreciated neat textbook answers explaining how these crimes were permitted. The real solutions to the questions they appear afraid to ask are in science books throughout the land. It can be seen in glossaries under "Second Law of Thermodynamics,"...i.e., Things left to themselves deteriorate.

The FBI had talked with my sister. They asked me to forget all my past to help them arrive at their forgone conclusion. They wanted me to forget when we reached out for help, and the lady from CPS called mom to ask if we were being abused. I remember it well; mom assured the lady from CPS it was not the case. She no more than hung up the phone when she started beating me. Grandma used to tell us that even a broken clock is right twice a day. I knew they had an outside chance of getting this right. I observed clocks also had complex inner workings. The fact they would not openly reveal their workings caused me concern. They came with questions. They did not have answers.

It would be easy for me to repeat, "He made a choice, and now he must pay for it." It would be acceptable to admit he was raised in an environment that incubates that behavior. Some things are known today that were denied yesterday. The FBI lady wanted to understand what permitted such an unacceptable behavior to manifest itself. They called because they wanted to know what I thought, as long as what I thought could support or add support to what they claimed to know. It is easy to look at distant situations and report on what. If one wishes to arrive at the correct perspective, there remain instances where one must seek the why of what. Our system does not acknowledge that abused people question authorities. One of America's biggest lies is the lie of there being equal rights under the law.

Chapter 19

Many in the queen's court would tell you that Dad died because he destroyed his liver. I cannot imagine how he made peace with the fact of his death while his body was craving a distorted form of death and recalling the throes from his time of service. I understand he drank. I have never seen him lift that glass. What may surprise some is that Dad did not drink until after he left the service and years after he had married mom. Some in the family from outside the house would proclaim he started drinking because he fathered a special needs son. These tend to believe such makes one less of a man. You may accept that answer if you wish. According to the Queens, it was a prevalent answer for his generation. I, however, saw my dad's compassion toward children in need. I noticed when he'd come home on a bad drunk. I know he'd beat my brother. You are free to accept the textbook answers. I don't. I think mom's inability to stand against the queens led to his drinking.

During WWII, he was in the Navy. He talked of his meeting a sitting president during his time in the service. What he would not speak of was the sinking of his ship. Others told of their surviving for days out in the deep the best they could. As his mind faded in and out of reality, he unfolded accounts of screaming men being pulled into that grave. He spoke of being awakened by the cries of others being devoured by the sharks. Dad would not talk of being one of the forgotten. Once, near the end, he told how it felt like they were pulling him apart when they took him from that grip of death. He also has a funny account of how he sunk the Bismarck with a bayonet after swimming for hours to do it. History does not tell of those falling from being the best to one forgotten. It does not record how they became the ones in a Navy hospital and then to one denied and betrayed. He told of the torment of wondering if he was rescued. At times, he felt the presence of those who remained with the ship. He said existence is a vast grave while telling how the War ended before he healed. When the Navy doctor declared him fit, he was honorably discharged without honorably being supported.

Dad had a steel ankle bone and a metal plate in his head. He had several wounds to remind him of his time of service. What was not received was support. He went through the proper authorities, explaining his migraines and other side effects. His symptoms were determined not to be accepted as war-related until after he died. When he died, the Navy sent two men to the house to settle the matter with his fourteen-year-old son (me), who didn't have any of the facts or a clue about life in general. I did not grasp how there are no genuinely unrelated events. I had been ordered to sign the check over to mom, or else the War took another life as the house plotted to create another victim. Dad's first name is not given in the list of the surviving crew of the Indianapolis. However, a few crewmembers came by the house to meet with the son of another so-called survivor. Dad never received any aid for his wounds. He was denied medical help by the people he fought to save, and he never stopped complaining that the sun was baking his head.

Today, they understand such is the body's reaction to dissimilar metals. Dad told me he began to drink to ease the pain, and it just got out of control. He was not proud of what he had become. Some would say dad lost his chance at life in that watery grave. Some view him as surrendering his life when he filled his glass. Some claim he lost his life's fight when his mother died. Yet there remains a perspective that shows we all come into this world screaming from the fear of death's pursuit. You may wish to claim because I am his son, I am blinded to the facts. I simply want to remind you of others we seem to have forgotten.

All the effects concerning Agent Orange are still not released. Could the reason be it is cheaper to settle the accounts once the overtaken survivor's death process is completed? No one can claim that the proper medical treatment would not have made an enormous difference in his life. No one knows if he ever would have started drinking. No one knows if they would have had children. There are lots of things that no one knows. Yet there remain a few things we do, such as some have given their all to this country. People this country has betrayed and wish to be forgotten. That is wrong, no matter how you slice it.

After dad died, I rode my bike past the dirt path he rented a place on. There was a note taped to the mailbox which bore his address. It was a message from the man who robbed me of his tools. In addressing it, he used dad's name but gave him the title "The King of Toe Path. He later told me my sister's dad had sold him my tools. He claimed he had misplaced the receipt. I can still hear her telling mom she told him, "If he wanted the tools bad enough to steal them from a dead man's kid, he could keep them."

Why would a man in such an exalted position leave a note taped to the mailbox of someone they knew had been hospitalized for the last five and a half months? He wished to appear superior. You may believe he did it for whatever reason you like. The man wrote the note for me. He wanted me to realize there is no equal justice under the law. He remained unchallenged by the house in the theft of the tools and the epitaph he branded on dad's existence. Dad was named after another prominent southern city; however, it is in North Carolina, not Mississippi.

Chapter 20

Across the street from the house stood a white Cape Cod with a light green roof. The old man in this house had been a real live rocket scientist. His wife played the piano and gave lessons to children about our neighborhood. The house to his left, if exiting the front door, was the house I went to when I went back and announced the house was on fire. Still, the old man and his wife, in Cape Cod, were good people. He helped me several times. I studied him because he worked on his lawn with the strangest tools. He knew carpentry. He built an arbor for his grapes and a greenhouse for her flowers. I wanted to learn more about what he'd put in their garden. He built lawn benches and lawn furniture for their house. They had two fruit trees.

One day, he was doing something on his porch while working. He had a ruler, which unfolded. I was fascinated by the thing. He handed it to me, almost begging me to be careful. Skillfully, I held it in trembling fingers and carefully snapped it while trying to get the darn thing to unfold. He did not raise his voice or hand. He told me not to worry because it was his fault. He said he should have shown me how to use it. He gave me the broken pieces so I could practice.

They were old before I was born. They never had a kid, but they had two perfectly pruned cherry trees and a beautiful lawn and garden. I saw him outside one evening. He was up in his tree, so I went over to help while explaining to him how much I liked cherries, as though the juices running off my chin wouldn't have been a hint enough. When he finished picking for the evening, he told me I could gather all I wanted and that he did not want me to climb a ladder. I asked how I could get the ones up top, trying to convince him to let me use his ladder. He remained firm and told me, "Anyway, you can. You'll figure it out." When he came home the following evening, one of the trees was on its side, and I was busy picking cherries from what used to be its top. Not a crossword was spoken. Not a moment of rage was detected. He loved the fact that I used my saw. He only came to ensure I was alright but loved that I figured it out. He missed the tree, but he loved that I solved the problem. He was a nice old man and loved that I thought outside the box. He used the experience to teach me to look past a moment's desires. He built something in the space where the tree once stood. I cannot recall what.

The year before my brother died, he was my homeroom and math teacher. He retired from the aerospace industry to become an Advanced Algebra teacher. He asked me to stay behind one day. After we were alone, he told me he had my back. He did. He would listen and sometimes ask questions to help me come to a better conclusion. Still, mostly, he listened and did what was in my best interest.

The old man came out of retirement to work in a school system. In his spare moments, he listened to and looked after the kid across the street who destroyed his folding ruler and cut down his cherry tree. The old man taught in a political system and took a position beneath him. He remained as long as I was at the school. Then he retired again. Still, he never stopped teaching me. He also demanded to be my homeroom teacher and warned me that the school did not like me but promised to have my back.

Chapter 21

I called my uncle, who took me in after I escaped shortly before he passed. He told me his body was betraying him, and his wife was out at the base shopping in the PX (Military grocery Store). Their kids were grown, and his granddaughter was in another room doing something. I asked how he was doing. He confided; he did not think he'd be around much longer. Then he reminisced and started reminding me of things we used to do when we were younger. When I was a child, I used to run past him after saluting and calling him Sir. He'd act like it bothered him as he'd swat me with the flyswatter while exclaiming, "Don't call me Sir; I work for a living." My aunt would get after him for hitting me with that 'dirty ole flyswatter.' We would all laugh, and I'd be at it again.

I remembered our camping trips. This uncle used to take us out to bark at us about the proper way to set up base camp. One person in our group was well-known for escaping tasks. She would wander off or hide behind the tarps, which became our camper's latrine. On one trip, my uncle decided he had had enough. It wasn't long after we had arrived that my uncle announced the lavatory was set up. Remember that the man was in the Army for 34 and 1/2 years. He had a few crank-type telephones from the army surplus so we could talk from tent to tent. Unknown to us, he had rigged up the toilet seat, which wasn't more than an old toilet seat attached to a five-gallon bucket. When that certain someone disappeared, my uncle gathered us around him using his hand signals, which motioned us to be quick and quiet. We seemed to be awaiting this event forever before he finally picked up that old crank phone and gave the crank a whirl. We heard her yell about the time she appeared. I think she thought she was a bit until she spotted us laughing. I am sad to report she was not the only one who received one of his cranks, though she was the first. The trick was too good to discard. There may be some who believe such schemes to be harsh. All I know is those are among my favorite memories of him.

After we talked for a while, he told me I was a good kid and then told me it wasn't my fault. His mother didn't like him either. He told me I shouldn't worry about him. He said he was ready to go, had a good wife and three beautiful children, and it was time. He then called me by my given name, "Jackson ____ _____, life without death becomes absurd; live life to the fullest."

I remember walking around the Square with my uncle. Some woman ran up to us and demanded to know how many babies I'd killed. My uncle tapped me to let me know he was fielding that question. He squared off and looked that woman dead in the eyes. Swelled up as only a retired sergeant could and said, "Lady, I have fought in every War, conflict, and police action this county has been in from WWII through Vietnam. I have been in some of the most brutal battles mankind has ever known. I have served my country as an artilleryman for over thirty years. I taught math at West Point. I want you to know that I have sent thousands upon thousands of rounds down range in battle. I'd hate like hell to think I've wasted the taxpayer's money and missed every G** D** time." He looked over and gave a look. I snapped to attention and awaited his cadence before we marched off. I do not know what happened to the woman; she may still be there for all I know, but we've moved on.

One time, my uncle and his family visited the house when I was receiving some treatment. It got rough. An adult in his late thirties or early forties who had married one in the queen's court was pretending to defend his wife so he could slug me. He told me he was going to "kick my ass." I told him to pack his lunch "because it wouldn't be a picnic." My uncle left the kitchen table and came out to introduce himself. That jerk settled down and sheepishly found his way to a corner. My uncle looked over at me, then he nodded and asked," Why don't you hop in the truck and come out to our place? I have things to do and could use your help." Not a word was said about what was happening. No questions were asked concerning my willingness to fight a man twice my age. There was no mention of the kicks to my ribs or the punches I had endured. There was a simple invitation. In many ways, I never returned to the house.

There are things people are willing to rob existences of so they may briefly live. I was never treated as my uncle's son, though I was accepted as his son. He would defend me. He would take time to talk with me. He taught me boundaries, and his rules were immutable. When he would get going to give one of the lectures that parents give, sarcasm would flow freely from his lips. His face would turn bright red and look like it would explode. Veins would appear through his temples. The capillaries in his cheeks would appear to become purple. Still, I knew that man would have died defending me. While I was talking to him on the phone that last time, he told me he was sorry he should have done more. The man who took me in. The man who rescued me. The man who allowed me to make my mistakes and guided me into what I've become wished he'd done more. He regretted not kicking down the house's door. However, he did what he thought to be right at the time. The depth of the degradation in the place will never be laid bare. There remain crevices in its darkness that we will never be viewed. Still, it is painful to pull yourself and loved ones from the equation and do what is best for all people.

The Respectable Stranger knew this and called it wholesome care when warning the nation, "*If ever this vast country is brought under a single government, it will be one of the most extensive corruptions, indifferent, and incapable of wholesome care over so wide a spread of surface. Popular government' He explained, depended on wholesome care exercised by elected leaders; healthy governance requires that human liberty be maintained as the ultimate political value.'*" When T. Jefferson was our minister in France, their

Revolutionary War erupted. Of it, he said, "*God forbid that we should be twenty years from such a rebellion; what country can preserve its liberty if their rulers are not warned from time to time that their people reserve the right of rebellion.*"

I recall when the youngest queen came out to my uncle's place with her new love. They came trying to provoke something. They began with their typical complaints. Basically, claiming my behavior was unpredictable and sometimes mean. I am sure this was their view; I had been taught never to attack when expected. I struck when I chose. I also refused to allow them to know when their blows hurt. My purpose in fighting was to deliver the message that someday I would stand. I recall believing I needed to do something so over the top that they'd never have anything to do with me. Soon after this belief was accepted, their physical abuse stopped. Mainly because the queen had run out of willing contestants to come and dance.

My uncle used to tell people that I never looked for trouble; I'd just pull it from my hip pocket, throw it down, and tell it to dance. He'd tell me I could push through most of this world's doors until I discovered one that needed to be pulled. Still, after being hit by baseball bats, skillets, belts, and electrical cords, I was made painfully aware that sleep could be interrupted by someone pouncing on me as another kicked me in the ribs or stabbed me with an icepick, made fist lose the desired effect. I did not go into these situations thinking I would return unharmed; I went in thinking

I'd hurt their bodies and then decorate the cake. I left traces of pain to remind them of where they'd been and warn others to stay away. I knew where to land blows to cause them to urinate blood for weeks.

Their mental abuse continued, but I was out of the house. They could no longer physically reach me. I was somewhat protected, having only to return for brief visits. I returned after work past midnight to sleep and was out by six AM. I went to school, to work, then to the house to try and sleep. I would have been at my uncle's place if I had had a few moments. The banter of the house was unreal. I was the common enemy. If I chose to fight, it was to hinder them, or that would probably be the house's unbiased opinion. The reality was I fought back to obtain a goal of my own. I desired to live. I saw in my father's death the plight his running had delivered. I knew well the pathway of silent sorrows. I also saw in glimpses from the man who once controlled industry that if life is only about the moment, it's an illusion, and reality lies breathless in its grave.

Before entering the tenth grade, I took the Army entry exam. I decided to do my time and be gone. I volunteered for the safety of war to escape the house, realizing there was no end to death's cycle. The only way to endure was to remove me from the equation. Existence became a sad, sick game, but I had already gone. I permitted my mind to be elsewhere. The days during this period encapsulate the others. All could have been captured by the same stroke of the painter's brush, excluding the days of death's awakening.

Chapter 22

I was biding the time when someone I knew came by telling me of his new employment. He came by the high school to offer me a job. We went to the establishment, and the manager hired me to help handle some trouble. I was offered the position before we entered the establishment. It appeared some teens were getting loud and causing a scene in this establishment. Because the cops were notorious for being slow at best in coming to their aide, we were employed to help keep the establishment clean.

The only thing they had me cook was french fries, and even that did not happen often. There was this one old guy who would only give me his order and money. For whatever reason, the man only dealt with me. Then, the manager took a position with the railroad. He and our new Z-28 moved away. The new manager was some woman who expected me to cook, clean, and do the same stuff the others did. I moved on. The place closed within a year. Then, questions began to surface throughout their Queendom about never seeing me on dates. Little snide remarks would occur to get a response.

I liked a girl in the seventh grade and allowed the house to know it. I was getting ready for the school's dance. Mom tried to help me. My sister returned from college and took me to the florist, where I was instructed to purchase her corsage and boutonniere. In the winter of seventh grade, I was chased around the house while trying to dress by my oldest sister with a camera snapping pictures. Pictures of me in my underwear started being shared with outside-the-house family members. My sister told me I was cute and that someday, my wife would cherish those pictures. I told them the next girl they would know about would be my wife. It was a true statement, except they knew about the girl I dated while in the Army, but only because she moved in across the street. How could anyone introduce someone they cared about into the house?

My next job after the fast-food joint was at the Country Club. I started out washing dishes. If you wish to know the dirt on people of a community, except a job where you mingle amongst its inebriated rich. Not the wealthy. Not the ones who have it. They are financially secure in their futures, but the up-and-comers: Wealthy people believe they are set for whatever life throws their way. They haven't the need nor the desire to play the games to try to prove their worth to others. The rich, however, are trying to climb their ladders. Don't become deceived by their fears of falling; these people, though often soft-spoken, can be brutal. When you're amongst them, don't bother listening to the men. Their stories never change except in names. "Did you know she was...? I'd like to...My position is...." If you want the dirt, listen to the women. They'll tell you who is doing what to whom. Who is getting a divorce? Who is the cause? Who is keeping the property, and who is holding the money? They do not merely know how to get the best deals.

They know what the actual cost of accepting the agreement is. If you desire to see the dirt in your community, listen to the inebriated banter of rich women. Yet when these women talk, things take on new names. My dad was a common drunk; their loved ones were intoxicated or struggling with a social disease. My dad couldn't hold his liquor; their loved ones were social drinkers who just that once needed to be driven home. My dad cheated when he visited the whore house; they were simply having an affair or frequenting each other's homes at opportune moments, or perhaps they frequented houses of ill repute. I saw how they would use someone until they had enough and discard them. The women they visited had fallen or become trapped in the oldest profession. Dad's women had no other choice, nor had they any other means to survive.

I liked knowing what cars the up-and-comers drove. Occasionally, they could be seen on our side of town. Half of our town was dry, but our side could never muster the votes needed to keep it from becoming more than slightly inconvenient to our rich. Don't be deceived; our town was the county seat and one of the wealthiest cities in the world according to its population-to-money ratio. One out of every four homes was said to be a millionaire's lodging, but many rich people only acted like they had money. They would jump into debt and swim to keep above the debt, hoping to get out before drowning. The people with money seldom flaunted it unless they were loaded and had to give it to Uncle Sam. Where there is money, there are crimes. If these crimes are committed by people presumed to have money, there are translucent cover-ups.

Chapter 23

When I was a kid, there was a single man, about sixty-seven, or at least he was in my mind and lived across the field. He was a scary guy. Or he was to children in the neighborhood. His beard never came in, yet he was never clean-shaven. His face was full of nubs, which could have become whiskers and were mostly shades of gray, but a few still lingered, holding on to being black. This made his face appear like he stood too close to a fire and needed to wash the soot off. He'd set up sawhorses in the back of his house and placed plywood on them to make tables. The rumor was he was related to someone important in town, someone who had money, not that he ever lacked from not having his own. Near the spot he'd sit up the tables in his backyard was the door to a root cellar or bomb shelter. Whichever it was, it was beneath his house. The screams which came from beyond that door will haunt the memories of kids from our neighborhood forever.

The guy would go fishing, and after cleaning his fish, he would hang these little balloon-like things on the hog wire fence between us. Grandma said they were just fish lungs, but my brother told me fish didn't have lungs; they had gills. They were nasty little things, and I never figured out why he would take the time to dry them. The man was scary, but he got rid of the neighborhood's stray cats. He used to try to lure kids into his cellar, but we dared not go. He'd make paper kites for other kids out of newspapers and strips of scrap wood he'd rip to size. We would never accept anything from him. He tried to talk with us. I was afraid of him because the kids coming from his place would run to their houses and were usually crying. All the guys from our neighborhood kept away from him. Stray dogs did not like the man. The cops would drive past his place slowly, but they never stopped. There was plenty of rumor concerning him. Still, none of us in the house ever asked him anything because we did not genuinely desire to know. Sometimes cops would come to just hang out. Someone should have instructed our undercover cops to lose that lean and cop walk.

Once my brother and I tried to snare a bird using the box, stick, and string method. Things could have gone better. It didn't matter which cereal or left-over vegetable we snuck to try and lead one under the box; the birds were getting away. We were out in our field when my brother spotted a squirrel at the base of one of our walnut trees. He unfolded our plan. I ambled towards the tree, pretending to want to capture the squirrel. He snuck up behind the tree. Our goal was working. When I got too close, it ran to the back of the tree. Before I knew it, my brother started screaming. When he came around the tree, I thought he had it, but the truth is, it had him. It bit him and was not letting go of that sweet meat between the thumb and pointer finger. My brother was running around. I was running around trying to catch him to help free him of the beast. However, my brother was faster. He tried to kill the thing with whiplash, but the squirrel would not let go. My brother was running and screaming, and I was running and calling while sending up prayers, thanking God that He allowed my brother to capture that killer. We were not paying attention to where we were running, and somehow, we found ourselves in the creepy guy's yard. Our running stopped. We became silent. My brother grabbed that squirrel and yanked its teeth from his hand. That squirrel is the first animal in space. We were back in our yard before our shadows knew we had left. We poured peroxide and painted his wounds with that red burning stuff. We were discovered. My brother had to see the doctor to get a series of shots. We never ventured into the neighbor's yard again, although, for a little while, the guy tried to get me to. Dad put an end to it. I heard him tell someone he told guy if anything happened to me, he'd hold him accountable. Occasionally Dad would come to the sliding barn doors of the horse barn and stare at the guy so we could play. That guy would go back inside. He did not live there very long after dad's talk. Some blind woman who made the other kids read her the newspaper moved in. I was unwilling to sound out any of the big words. She was unable to prove that I could. I was only chosen once. That Lady learned the neighborhood's kids by voice and the sound of their gait.

When I was a kid, we could tell which decade a house was built in by the size of its front porches. After the men returned from WWII, people didn't plan for company coming, sitting, relaxing in the evening's breeze enjoying each other's company. Therefore, houses' porches gradually became smaller until they disappeared altogether.

I've never trusted newspapers. It felt like they only contained a version of the truth, and too often, it was a version of the reality they were told to sell. Capture the battlefield, create the news. Our first and second presidents did not see eye to eye with our third president. But the third was the man rumored to have pinned, "We hold these truths to be self-evident...." The first was permitted the privilege of writing his own history, which allowed talking about our third president's relationship with a specific slave. I found it interesting George forgot he owned Martha's half-sister. It was probably an oversight, or so I was told. I was also told it should not have been in my report. Still, her half-sister was never listed in any of his household records. Martha's sister was half Cherokee and half Black. She was not granted freedom until the Washington's died. During that period, the one-drop rule was in effect. How is it that Martha was considered to be white? Money and power alter facts.

Once my brother stayed with a couple. The woman owned our town's dance studio. He seemed to be happy when he lived there. He was dating a girl who was older than himself. Her dad owned the local paper; I'd heard she wanted me to visit after he died. Mom told her she could not allow it. I needed to learn how to reach her. The opening, which allowed him to walk out, had closed. Eventually, she moved away, but still, from time to time, I pondered what it would have been like getting to know her.

After my brother died, I heard rumors of a massive drug bust. The newspaper covered the police report and robberies. My job at the Country Club covered the news and the politicians. People were protesting the War, which our local paper called a police action. Our flag was being burnt. America was being awakened from its self-afflicted unconsciousness. Four college kids were killed up the road by the National Guard, and Crosby, Stills, Nash, and Young wrote a song about it. I was marking time, waiting for the clowns to pass. I have never really trusted clowns. They come out performing their antics, trying to overcome being a sideshow. They paint on those faces, yet their painted faces can't disguise the sorrow in their eyes. I distrusted clowns for the longest time, unable to get past the fact they tried to lie, not realizing the biggest lies we ever hear are ones we tell ourselves. This led me to discover that when the masses to revolt, those who seek power tremble.

After my brother passed, I started mowing lawns during the warm months of spring. There was a couple up the street I mowed for. The Lady was very good looking. The couple had two small children. The Lady and I would talk. We shared truths about our stolen childhoods. Said she ran away to marry her husband when she was sixteen. He said they would not have children until she finished high school. She told me her grades greatly improved once freed from her past. She told me her husband was crazy about her, but his father didn't care much for her. She didn't know what they'd do if it were not for the pension left them from his grandfather's estate. He had to take a position elsewhere because his father wouldn't allow him to work out of his family's company. Anyway, she was a lovely lady, and we became friends. Sometimes, when I mowed, she'd lay out. These were friendly people, and nothing ever happened between us.

One day, while I was mowing the front, she was lying in their back-yard. However, it was a corner house, so their back looked more like a side yard from the main street. Though the Lady didn't like to mow, she kept the lawn fertilizer and their flower beds, and bushes trimmed perfectly. I knew it would have significantly aided my ability to acquiring other lawns if I got that lawn. She and I would talk. Sometimes she'd ask if I'd like a soda after I finished their yard, and we chatted while drinking our sodas. It was easier for me to talk with her because she didn't want anything.

We understood what our words couldn't say. Anyway, the Lady was lying out, and this time, when I passed, she raised onto her elbows to ask if I'd like a soda. Before I could answer, we heard a crash ahead of us. I did not hear breaks squeal or another car, just the sound of the cop car ramming into a parked car. The road by her home was four lanes wide though it only was designated for two. She said it might be better if we went into the garage. Once inside, she excused herself to change and bringing us the drinks.

As we entered the garage, we heard the siren come on. We stayed in the garage. Trying to remain out of sight of the cops and firemen we heard coming. Once the police had finished their investigation, I slipped out. The next day the paper told how the cop had lost control while in a high-speed pursuit. It went on to state they went door to door trying to find witnesses, but no one along that stretch of road had seen a thing.

I never heard anything other than the cop hitting the parked car; not even his breaks were heard. The only black marks made from the crash were those made by the parked vehicle when it slammed against the curb. I told a friend about it. His dad interjected after I finished telling my friend, "You'll forget your version if you know what's good for you." The paper a little while later reported how the veteran officer was injured in the crash after losing control of his cruiser during the high-speed pursuit. He was expected to make a full recovery. It also said he would be eligible to receive compensation for the injuries he had sustained. She never laid out on that part of their lawn again. I mowed their lawn until they moved into a ranch-style house out in the country. Their new location was out of the city's corporate limits. She told me her husband had to put in for a transfer right before they moved. They were gone before summer ended.

Chapter 24

During the summer between my second and third grade, our school hired a new, single, young third-grade teacher. We were her first assignment after completing college. She was a nice-looking lady. The older boys said, "She was built or put together well." She was nice but had a different style of dressing than the more senior teachers. Her shoulder-length sandy blond hair was free and not put up as the other teachers. Somehow it came to the attention of somebody in the system that she was also going to have a baby. The word got around. The playground began to mumble about her. I know she wasn't the first unwed pregnant teacher in our town's history, but still, they removed her from their system over the Christmas break because of someone being concerned.

This thing they replaced her with was mean, old, and ugly as the losing bare-knuckle fighter. She had big thick heavy horned rimmed glasses. She didn't shave her legs or armpits. She put her hair in one of those beehive things somebody talked women into wearing. Those beehives looked wrong from the back; it looked like apples, oranges, grapes, and other fruits would start popping out at any moment. Her glasses were so heavy they kept sliding down her nose. She kept them on a chain she wore about her chinless neck to prevent them from shattering from the fall. That woman yelled all the time. Well, maybe not all the time, but if she wasn't screaming, she was blowing her darn whistle. I could not understand how she got the position. Perhaps her best qualification was an unwritten guarantee she would not show up pregnant. I must admit, I did not care for her. Her gigantic owl eyes filled those coke bottle glasses. Those eyes didn't even look in the same direction. Her head swiveled on a tiny, thick wrinkle between two padded shoulders. When she appeared to be looking straight ahead, she would yell at me for doing something off to the side. I never knew where she was looking. She wore those old ladies' shoes with those low, thick heels that were only two inches high and the evil which also wore them. Her leg hairs would pop out of her support hose, which could not hide the bumps and ridges the varicose veins formed across her legs.

The house out of concern for its captured boy had it vary own wanting woman. That mean nasty lesser queen. She earned her living teaching snakes to hiss. She woke to a different world every day. The woman could be divorced on Friday and married Saturday morning. She did it: Twice. She was the talk of the down and outers about town during her divorces. The woman was something she knew every crack in the sidewalk and bar stool where women went for a few moments of fame.

During my third-grade year, our school system fired an outstanding teacher who liked children. They fired her because they claimed she was a "wanton woman." I looked the term up in the dictionary. By the time I finished the third grade, the house had gone out and secured our wanton woman. It and had her come over regularly to steal our nourishment and doctor our food to ensure we three boys would steer clear of all such women.

Even my retarded brother made the correct choice. I remember when she came over to tell us she and that uncle would not be married much longer. She explained how one of them would no longer be related. My brother chose her ex-husband. The way she explained it, he thought we could choose which one we kept.

Chapter 25

The house was a few blocks from where the soapbox derby was held. I used to look forward to the fourth. I would go and look over the cars kids from all around would try to convince others they built. In the back alleys of the town, you could listen to discover who built the cars after the race. It was always the same guy who created the best ones in town. He also made the best chopper forks. He would weld them together using tear-dropped steel, which he placed on an old springer front end. He sent his creations out to be chromed. His work was exact. There was never a seam to be found, and they looked like they grew from their frames. His location was also very convenient. It was a few blocks from our junior high school. The man knew how to twist and bend metal. Kids from far and wide came to purchase his custom work.

I went to the soap box derby races to see his creations and the crashes. I would cheer for anyone I liked but cracked jokes about the others. On the fourth, I could chill and kill time. I did so until it was time to make the cross-town walk to the park. Across the levy, we would search for a nice spot to stretch out to watch the fireworks.

Along the derby's course, on the right side of the street, which they ran while going down the hill, stood a white-painted brick and lap-sided house. This place had a cutaway hidden drive, which looked like it was attached to the basement. On the fourth, I would walk across the edge of its lawn, only near the curb. At all other times during the year, I kept a safe distance from that house. My handyman's uncle painted houses in that area for extra cash. This house never seemed to need his help, but I never caught anyone working on it. Its outward appearance was kept up. It was a nice-looking house with a well-maintained lawn; still, something was haunting about the place.

My uncle, the career soldier, once again returned to Vietnam. His family was stationed at the base, which houses the 101st airborne. Since Christmas was approaching, people in the extended family circle were asking what I wanted for Christmas. I gave each and every one of them the same answer. I told them I wanted the billfold. Now, to aid your understanding, there is a saying that I cut my teeth on. "You ain't a man till your daddy tells you." I did not care what color it was. I was not concerned about whether it was a bi-fold or a tri-fold. As this was going on, I heard the talk about the house. I realized plans were being formed about us going to Fort Campbell to celebrate the holidays with his family. When mom was talking to my guardian aunt once, she handed me the phone to speak with her long-distance. After doing so, she left the room. My aunt asked what I wanted for Christmas. I told her I wanted the billfold.

Some ears of the house could never hear what was said. Others knew I did not want a billfold; I liked the billfold. The problem was that dad was too busy dying to be aware of his obligations. People with faces kept coming up to me, asking if I was sure all I wanted was a billfold. Repeatedly, I assured them the billfold was all I wanted. They kept mumbling things about this or that which they thought I might desire. I guess their questions were their way of trying to understand, as they were trying to prepare for dad's death and the consequences. In truth, these relatives were already dead to me. I was already numbed by their acts. Their timing stunk. I was already through with them.

Finally, the day awoke. We piled into our car and drove to the fort. Our oldest sister, who considered herself an adult, stayed with the adults and tried to act like she was everyone's parent. It was Christmas Eve when a knock came on my aunt's back door. A soldier's young wife, whose husband was deployed to the police action, came seeking help. She had purchased a trike but needed help to get the thing together. I went with her to help. Before long, I had boxes of items, bikes, and wagons to try to assemble by morning.

Shortly before sunup, I reenter my aunt's place. My head barely hit the pillow when I was awakened to eat cereal and open the presents. Our relatives had all come by to give us gifts they had purchased for them and included the small things they had for us. My aunt gave me my present while she whispered in my ear, "This one is from your uncle. He sent it to me and told me to let you know he bought it for you." I don't know what ever happened to the other boxes handed to me that Christmas. I cannot tell you if they were ever opened. They were all the same size. All I know is they were rejected. I can also tell you the opposite of love is not hate. The opposite of love is indifference, which resides in a cold, shallow place that is just deep enough to swallow yourself.

Still, all things being considered, it is my favorite childhood memory of Christmas.

When I was a kid, a lady rode her bike around town. This Lady lived her existence out in the weather for all to see. Though her skin had become golden from the sun's glow, which is if it is proper for one to say skin that covers a sorrow-filled existence is golden. Her skin did not show a trace of the furrows which the sun usually gifts existence. She wasn't covered with freckles, nor did she have blemishes. Her skin was colored with the soft, clean rays of youth. Her eyes were piercing green. She was a medium blond. The sun had bleached out strands of color from her wind-tossed hair. Her teeth were white and straightened. Her overall appearance was clean but never orderly. The tops of her socks seemed to drop and rarely matched. She was not ugly, nor would I say she was pretty. She was not cute; however, to me, she was alluring. I had heard others comment on her through their cruel jokes of youth, displaying they were the children of those who would not understand. When I first became aware of her, she was just some lady riding a bike. As I studied, I began to appreciate the grace and strength she displayed as she glided through our neighborhoods. She had a silent power that I felt many could not view.

There is strength in one daring to be themselves regardless of the consequences.

While studying her, I discovered our worlds are not defined by individuals, for they can be determined by our illusions of knowledge. Though her bike seemed plain and straightforward, such was far from the truth. Her bike had a basket attached to its handlebars. I cannot recall her ever carrying anything in it. She came by the house on Thursdays, for such was the day the trash men came. As she glided through our streets, she would look to see what people had thrown out, but I don't recall her ever stopping, touching, or taking anything. As far as many were concerned, this Lady did not talk. Her speech was acceptable whenever I spoke with her. Her parents were killed in a car crash. She was being controlled by her mother's parents, who lived on a gigantic farm in a massive house. Her grandfather had other people who did his farming/ranching and the general upkeep of the estate. He owned some business and was said to be rolling in the lute. Sometimes, the street would claim she'd been better off if they passed also. Those who thought they knew said the state would commit her and take her fortune unless the property and wealth were protected.

The Lady did not speak about such things. She aimlessly peddled about upon her two-speed bike. Folks claimed her to be another sad case of love gone wrong. They would tell how she once was in love with a hired hand. They were all a little younger then and naiver. The young man went to the grandfather requesting permission to marry her. People claimed that the old boy went nuts. They say some observed him walking about, explaining to the air that he had lost one girl by allowing it to happen. He was not about to let it happen again.

They tell how they eloped or how the couple was captured while they attempted to. They describe how the girl was carried back. For some reason, he had to run off and join the Army. While overseas, he became some kind of hero. They did not tell how he never married or why she thought of him while silently gliding through our streets. However, it gave her a welcoming smile as she talked to little kids. The fact that I was small for my age made speaking easy when she talked with me. I had heard them say she would just sit in her room and pine over that boy. They would tell how she refused to be seen at anticipated social events. They would say that since her capture, she refused to dress up or to even put on makeup. Some told a tale of her nearly dying from tick fever, which they claim she contacted during their escape. Those who said that version of her story seemed to like to warn others that love could do some amazing things. I believe her grandparents have passed by now. If so, the storytellers have discovered that though love can cover many flaws, once accepted, it fills a longing soul.

Chapter 26

If I was reticent, when my fix-it uncle came, sometimes I would hear mom and him talking in the kitchen. Usually, this happened when they thought I was asleep or gone. They sat and spoke at the table while drinking coffee and eating her homemade pie. If a meal was served for guests, we ate pie in the dining room and gathered about the long hand-carved table with the protected padding for its top. We heard from many a visitor that the table was beautifully crafted, but I never got to behold its craftsmanship. However, if a friendly relative came when the pressure wasn't so great, they would gather in the kitchen around the little round table to sample a slice or maybe two of mom's pies and coffee. When mom made pies, or we turned her homemade ice cream, we had visitors. I have been punished more than once for giving the snake eye to one of the queens for gobbling down the remaining pie before doctoring up all the remaining prepared food and then leaving. Not even the Queen or her court dared to doctor one of mom's pies. My staring at them would not bring the swings. The swings would come afterward when one of them would claim to have read my eyes. I do not know what my eyes said, but my thoughts were clear about a sow's inability to save a morsel for her litter.

At these times, mom and the guest gathered at the little kitchen table and reflected on old times. However, the time I was most interested in was about a time right before WWII ended. This was the time frame when they became young adults. Dad and my uncles all fought in the war. Mom and her oldest sister were old enough and worked at the Waco Glider factory. My mom and my aunts were Rosy the riveters. The wealthy in our town did not need to worry about their kids going to war; they simply paid the going rate to keep their children out of consideration. It was the poor and immigrants who fought this war. Rich people paid for some poor schmuck to take their son's place. It was one of these accounts I tried to hear. I was interested in a famous unsolved murder.

It seemed there once was an affair between one of the wealthy boys and one of the wives of a poor schmuck who went off to war. What intrigued me was that they made it sound like the father of the wealthy kid hired her husband to take his son's place so he would not figure out that his wife was cheating on him with his son. Somehow, after the soldiers returned, he discovered his wife's secret and confronted the wealthy boy. They said he tried to be understanding of his wife's needs, but as usual, a fight broke out. Somehow the schmuck was killed. The weapon was never discovered. Mainly because the wealthy child's dad owned the gravel company. If the weapon was mentioned, it was only to say the knife would never be found. Those two old gravel pits were later given to the city so the taxpayers could convert them into parks. The concrete company raped our land, robbed us of the beauty of the natural gentle sweeping of our countryside, and then returned their monstrous mess through some loophole used to cheat their way out of returning the land to a valuable property.

The adults around the table would tell how she told the wealthy boy they were through. They would say it as though they were almost quoting her, "She could not be with the man who killed her husband." (I remember wondering if she could be with another murderer.) They told how she was given the lovely house where the soapbox derby was held in exchange for her silence. They said how the wealthy man's son grew into one of the bigwigs in town. How his dad paid some poor fool to take his kids' rap and then encouraged the powers that be to pile on other charges to help them tidy up some loose ends. The part of the story I liked best was the payoffs. One of the payees became a prominent real estate developer. Our town's rags to riches story. One became the chief of police in a nearby city. The other guy became our very own straw boss mayor. That is the story I liked to hear about. I was fascinated by how they knew little details. They told how the wealthy lived by permitting others to pay their debts. They never spoke of anyone being outraged. They whispered it, but only out of the need to talk about the truth.

Sometimes, they would tell how one of the soldier's childhood friends, who had gone through the war with him, tried to go to the authorities, or perhaps he'd gone to the wrong command. The soldier died shortly afterward. The man lived through major battles and came home to die defending the truth in a city that had no need to hear it. He died below his child's bedroom window. His son was still clutched to his chest. According to the coroner's report, they'd tell how he had reentered their house to save his boy but died of smoke inhalation. Still, I heard talk, and they knew someone was paid to strike that match. Many believed they would have made it without the stray bullet hitting him.

The woman who was given the painted brick house remarried once. Her new husband was killed by a robber. They say she was hurt so bad she could never have children. Luckily, something scared the robber off. It must have been them pulling into the garage below the house. The robber killed her husband in a scuffle, trying to get away. The only thing the robber took was her husband's life and the baby she was carrying. They said she was beautiful when she was young. Some in my town used women and tossed them to the dogs when finished. It seemed these relatives believed some lives were not worth a plugged nickel.

The woman was left alone in her house with time to think.

The Queen and her court used to warn each other, "When someone marries for money, they'll earn every dime." This caused me to wonder what else they knew about the story. That Lady and the house disturbed me. Occasionally I would see her form peering out from behind the lace off-white curtains.

There was another prominent white house in our town. It was less lovely than the one she stayed in; it was also on a corner. It was the corner across from our park and graveyard. When I was younger, I used to see chickens run free there. It was a simple cracker box farmhouse that the city swallowed. Adjacent to the house was a parking area, and across from it was the ice skating rink. The rink was built by the man who once controlled our industry. People in town said the man loved ice hockey. When the old couple living in the farmhouse died, the city bought it or took it. They planned to give it to the high-school students as a place to hang out. They could go there and play music or relax. There was a cop assigned to this house. At that time, every school in town had a cop assigned to them. At the grammar school, these cops trained and recruited the crossing guards. They also played with kids on the playground. They assumed the high school students knew how to cross a street. I was just a kid in junior high who walked about seven miles to school and was ungrateful, according to the Queen and her court. The cops assigned to the schools were given charge of certain appropriate things. The High school cop supervised the white house. However, the one given this duty was also a man who supplied our city with a particular controlled substance, or so the rumor went. He also had a wife who had a lover. The cop killed her lover and tried to make it look like self-defense. When he went to prison, they tore the white house down. I know some details, but there was considerable talk about the Country Club kids not needing extra cash. The end result is they bulldozed the house to make room for another parking lot.

My brother used to hang out there sometimes. The Queen and her court used to talk about him being involved in the drug scene. They did not have a clue. They must not have known that I had to sit up with him the night mom brought him out of the hospital. They must not have known how I was told; if he went to sleep, he would die. They must not have known that after staying awake all night, when morning came, I went to school, where I had to act like nothing had happened.

After the car crash, there were all sorts of rumors and things being said. These things were never confirmed in a police report. Mom said she had enquired through what she considered safe channels and reported, "There was no truth to the rumors." He was killed instantly in the crash during a sudden downpour. I died instantly of a broken neck just a little from where I was fishing. To this day, I believe I heard the crash. I know I listened to the sirens. Our retarded brother was at the scene. He doesn't understand, but he is in the photo of their mangled car taken for the newspaper.

People began to ask questions while feeding me what they considered to be information. I would hear about the location of where he smoked his first joint and of all who were there. They always seemed to need to add themselves. Sometimes, these people would even know where he took his first shotgun from the bong. After such statements, they would begin the questioning. I never knew about that stuff. I learned about the field where wild pot grew. I knew about driving out of state to get some plants. I knew how they separated the seeds, and it was sometimes cut with tea. I learned about the brick which grew when it was cut. I even knew the stuff he kept in the tin foil was stomping. I knew who hung out with him. I knew my way around, but I didn't know a thing about the first time he got high. I also knew their stories needed help because they changed each time they told them.

Shortly after his death, my retarded brother started running away. He would stick out his thumb and get rides to the *Heritage*. One time, he happened to meet *The Man in Black*. When Johnny first phoned mom, she hung up, thinking it was a prank. The next time, he told mom my brother was with June and him. Mr. Cash explained how they met him at the *Heritage* while my brother was looking for another singer, we had been told was our cousin. He explained to mom how they decided they best take him home. They told her he was fine and not to worry, saying they'd take care of her boy. Mom told them we'd be there as soon as we could. Johnny told her he had talked with my brother and knew money was tight. He said she should stay so she didn't miss any work and come pick him up on Saturday, which is what we did.

For a while, my retarded brother would not stay at the house. As soon as backs were turned, he would ride his thumb again. On one of our trips to get him, mom decided to make a vacation out of the return trip. They agreed that we would stop at everything related to Daniel Boone. They had signs that took people fifty miles off course to show a stump that once was a tree ole Daniel sprung a leak against. Finally, we came to the tourist trap of the Great Smoky Mountains. As we drove through, I was looking around. We were told we would eat at a nice restaurant and there would be no shenanigans.

I remember looking out my window and studying the people walking on the far side of the road compared to the shoeless Native Americans traveling along the dirt path on the other. I checked their facelessness as they tried to remain invisible while wandering. Their heads hung down as if they studied the dirt along the path. However, a girl who appeared to be about my age looked up. The girl's face needed washing, and the lower portions of her calves to her feet were darkened from her travels upon the path. Her dress had a faded flower print and a tiny tear at the bottom, but her eyes were open. She had big, bright, black eyes set wide apart. Her cheekbones were high, and she looked more alive than the others she traveled with. She caught me smiling as I looked at her and raised her hand somewhat shyly before halfway smiling back. That was until whoever held her other hand gave it a jerk to take her smile away. They could not dim the welcoming look she passed through the openness of her eyes. I remember watching her walk away until she was ripped from my sight. At about that time, mom announced she had found the restaurant. We were reminded of the conditions and walked towards its door. Again, we were warned it would be our last meal of the day. When the food came, those scolding me screamed while running from the table. They made quite a scene because of an inability to eat a trout that appeared to be staring at them.

Mom packed our lunch on the another of these trips to get my runaway brother. Near lunchtime, she told us to start looking for a place to picnic. We stopped at a clearing beside the road and ate our food on the grass. I liked looking at the scenery as we ate. After finishing the food, mom had a surprise for us. She had packed a watermelon in an ice chest.

Although we tried, we could not eat all that melon. Mom decided to leave it for the animals. My oldest sister started lecturing us about why it was not wise to do so. She ended her condescending tone by stating the heat would destroy the melon anyway. After listening to her, Mom told us to pick up our things and get in the car. While doing so, I observed mom chose her way to place that quarter slice of melon in the little stream, so it would keep and prove my sister wrong. When she came to the stream, she looked for just the right spot to leave the melon. Still, when mom found it, she bent over, placing it lightly in a small pool of water, ignoring the woods altogether. As she turned, we saw a bear and started to scream and jump. Mom hadn't seen it. However, she had no problem accepting how her feet took her once she spotted the bear. As we drove off, looking back, we saw why there weren't any tables or shelters erected on the spot where we stopped. When my sister saw why, she quit lecturing in mid-sentence, for she had chosen an overhang that was way over and looked barely hanging. Throughout the rest of that trip, we enjoyed the silence of our car tires' roar.

We tried to do everything, but my brother would not stay home. One day, quite by accident, we discovered the reason he ran. Our oldest sister was belittling him, and all at once, he burst into her browbeating, saying. "You don't have to sleep in that room with his empty bed; Jackson and I do." At first, I thought he was afraid of ghosts or that he missed our dead brother. Then he explained his reasoning by stating, "Grandma was warning us how death traveled in threes." He told her he wasn't giving death a chance to choose him. "When two more die, he'd stop running."

Mom told Johnny, and he called in my brother to talk with him when he again went to visit. Johnny promised he and June would stop in and see him at the gas station he worked at if he'd stop running away. The deal was offered and accepted. My brother retired his thumb. However, Johnny promised he and June would stop to visit. In truth, you would not believe the country stars who'd stop to talk or go fishing with my brother. He would show the stars how to enter through the back way of the gravel pit.

I discovered many things are different from what they appear to be. There were a lot of things about our sleeping little closed-eye town I could not understand. I understood that when I left the house, I felt protected by the company of the faceless strangers, who probably viewed me as faceless. There were several thousand in town, and I accepted I knew a tiny percentage of them. It was those which I knew, however, which stained my view of the town. I learned, out of self-defense, to study people, to understand the ones I could approach and the ones I needed to stay away from. A man's image still haunts my mind. He drove a big rig. The guys' eyes were cold, soft gray. Girls liked the way he looked, or so it seemed. I wasn't so put out that I didn't watch him. He had a way about him. He would park his rig off to the side of the road and jump out to walk to a nearby predetermined place. Sometimes, he walked the levy, but I never saw him with a fishing rod. The man was a walking contradiction. He did not look like the other truck drivers. He looked like a dad dating one of his daughter's friends. He seemed to be a magnet for young blonds because he came out of those places with one who would hop in his truck regularly.

Chapter 27

The house had carved moldings. Its doorways were trimmed by the finest local craftsmen of its period. The materials used were said to be too costly to be used by the housing industry today, for it was the best money could buy in its day. Her floors were sturdy. Fashioned from diagonal close-spaced true cut hemlock and covered by thick tongue and groove oak flooring. Still, despite all its elaborate features, my favorite room was the attic room. I had lost my share of change through the cracks in its unfinished floor. There was no heating, and we had to run power cords for space heaters, amps, stereo, and lighting. The ceiling, flooring, and walls were pine, and only one small window in a dormer from which I could gaze upon the world below. The queens believed we could not escape because eight feet is a good drop, but rain downspouts are an easy climb. It had never worn a coat of paint, and her unfinished pine flooring were smoothed by the foot traffic over time. Still, it was the only room that held potential. I could sit in her dormer, think, or watch the world rolling by. I could escape to the attic to search my head for answers. I could steal away and struggle while twisting and turning through the maddening events of the day. I could think and rearrange the details. I could exhaust myself reaching, reading, and searching for that right question to unlock the riddles of my tormented mind. Many times, I was awakened when an answer came.

Such images come from someplace high and from the right. They would lose color, fading slowly into gray. They departed low and towards the left. Someone once told me that people see images or dreams in black and white. In my mind, all my plans start from the same place. That place is where I sat in the old theater in the center of town. My dreams started from my seat as the red velvet curtains were pulled back. I remembered seeing those constantly expanding squares that came on before the movie previews.

Once, my brother and I were caught climbing the sheets we had tied together to enjoy our adventures. Mom was sitting at the foot of his bed when I entered the window. She was marking time with her foot and slapping dad's old belt firmly into the palm of her hand. Not a pretty memory. Have you ever had one of those spankings where you were spanked and lectured? I've never liked those. Her speech was too fast to understand, and she'd asked questions she didn't expect an answer. "Don't say another word... You better answer me when I am talking...I told you not! A! Word! Can you hear me?" Once I answered that, my ears were still ringing. It was not the correct answer, although it was a little better than, "Just go ahead and beat me a get this over with." I gave the signal to my brother so he could escape.

Once, the queen mother's granddaughter thought she needed something. Because of this imaginary need, her mother, a lesser queen, dropped her off. She returned for her moments before mom came in from work. The following morning, we were warned that the youngest Queen would babysit and receive payment. This being translated meant we would be doing without something minor, such as food, water, or shelter, so the princess could obtain whatever her little heart desired. If ever we went to grandma for something minor, say our finger was dangling from a threadlike piece of flesh, and asked for a nickel to buy a box of Band-Aids. We would be swung upon while being screamed at to get out of the house. She would call at the top of her lungs, "You stupid heathen, get out of this house," Look at the mess you're making for me. Blood dripping all over my clean floors. Do you think money grows on trees?" Often, I wondered if she knew the paper was a wood product. I also wonder why they were always her clean floors. I never saw her clean anything.

The Queen or her court did not necessarily have to ask for things. They needed only to allow their requests to be known. Whenever they thought they might need something, once grandma found out those needs, they were usually met. Our queen babysitter decided to try and bribe us with homemade cookies on this particular occasion. They couldn't let mom find out where the food money had gone. I do not know what it was she did wrong. All I know is that I couldn't eat the cookies. I am not saying they were not good tasting, nor am I saying I was not allowed. I am saying I could not eat the cookies. Believe me, I tried, but the darn things would not break. I tried and tested, and it became a challenge. No matter what I tried, I could not eat the cookie. Dunking them in milk wouldn't soften them. Then, a few days later, grandma took those cookies and tossed them back for the birds.

We had a field around the house with opossums, squirrels, stray dogs, cats, raccoons, birds, and nothing could eat those cookies. There was one old crow. A giant corn-fed one, which hopped around like a crippled old man. It swooped down and hobbled over to swipe a smaller cookie. It took it because crows like shiny things, and those cookies sparkled in the sunlight. It pecked at it for a while and then brought to holding it in its beak. That cookie was so heavy the crow had to abandon its first attempt at a takeoff. It hobbled to a landing once more and then back to its makeshift runway. It stopped for a moment to see if anything was watching. It then took more of a hopping, run-like approach, looking like a helicopter during one of those nose-down takeoffs. It kept its prize but barely cleared our hog-wire fence. Later, I had to go out and pick up the rest of the things before mowing the lawn. Grandma must have had visions of flying cookies screaming through the air and killing people.

Once, while we were going somewhere, I needed help remembering where.

Mom was driving, and grandma was riding shotgun with my baby sister riding between them. My brothers and I filled the back seat. We got a flat. Mom pulled over to change it out of traffic. She looked at the car as though she half expected the car to change its tire. Then came a puff of dust covering the car as we heard the sound of airbrakes. When the dust had settled, a man was seen climbing from his rig and asking mom if she needed help. That man wouldn't take money after explaining he had a little lady back home." wherever that was. Then he said, "sure hoped someone would help his Lady if she needed a hand. Through a smile, he explained that things come back around; he felt changing our tire increased her odds of getting help." He changed the tire in no time, but it felt like it took forever. I was nervous the entire time the trucker was there, though it didn't look like the walking contradiction's rig.

When my fix-it uncle found out about them not knowing how to change a tire, mom and my oldest sister had to listen to his lectures on "How to change a flat." When my sister heard enough, she started halfway, mockingly repeating the points with him. He said OK, let's go out and see you do it. That sentence silenced her. Because of her smart mouth, he had my sister go first. Mom helped her keep track of the lug nuts and handed them to her as needed; therefore, they both earned his approval of roadworthiness.

My friend next door and our friend from slab-town and I built forts in the small, wooded lot in the center of the horseshoe where his home butted against the tracks. These tracks divided us from slab-town. This was where the so-called poor people in town lived. Our neighbors and our property were separated from it by the DT&I Railroad and our forts. The other poor section was called Hollywood. It had a red-light district and backed into the Fairgrounds. It was separated from the different neighborhoods by levies that seldom held water. Things were happening in our communities because some people were losing their minds over skin colors. Anyway, my neighbor's strange dad came out and told us he did not think it was wise for us to play at the fort for a while. He told us the area of his yard, from the spider shrubs to the tracks, were ours to do with what we wanted. He told us we needed to stay close by because "Hatred didn't recognize age and blinded stupidity knew colors." We used spoons, toy shovels, and sticks to dig. Then scoured the area for scraps of wood. We built our new fort all summer.

After the winter's thaw, when the spring rains finally ended. It brought an invitation. The strange man came to my door with a smirk more than a smile overcoming his face. I had come to know the meaning of his expressions, so I got up knowing he came for me. As we headed toward his place, the man did not speak. When we went to a place where he was sure their home would no longer obstruct my view, he simply said, "We need your help." At first, I thought they were pulling the spider bushes out of their beds. When we got closer, I realized they were removing those bushes from our collapsed tunnels. Those beds were about a football field long and a third of the area-wide. Not a single spider bush remained above ground.

We three and the strange man worked at correcting it all weekend long. They fed us and gave us drinks. That weekend, we were all treated as though we were his kids. When we finished, everything was above ground, and he informed us how many cubic feet of soil he had purchased to reestablish his lawn's spider bush border. After doing so, he asked what we had done with all the missing earth. The others ratted me out, explaining that I had come up with a plan to fill old coffee cans with dirt and then pour it out on the flatbed cars of trains when they came by. They had to almost stop before going into the factory. Placing the dirt on the flat beds allowed the trains to scatter the earth for miles as they rocked to the rhythm of the rails; the soil simply fell through the slates unnoticed. The distance we placed between the dirt from the edge determined the distance the earth would travel before beginning its dismount.

Chapter 28

In the summer before my fourth-grade year, heavy machinery moved in along the tracts, in an area behind the AME Methodist Church in the southwest corner of Slab-town. That equipment and its men started changing my world. By the fall or the beginning of the school year, a brick home was being erected. It had a garden room in the middle of its entry and a concrete driveway complete with an attached two-car garage with enough extra space for storage all the way around. My friends and I had walked those tracts and taken a narrow, well-traveled path that once cut through the lawn of what would become a parsonage. We traveled that path to the shoe repair shop, where we purchased our chips, candies, and sodas and listened to the old men spinning their yarns or talking politics.

We walked the tracks looking for change, which had fallen, while men walked to the factory a few blocks further down the line. Some men must have cleared off places on the ties to leave some of their change, and we walked the tracks Monday through Saturday, hoping we'd find what they'd left.

After the new house became occupied, as we were walking the tracks, we noticed an elderly lady watching. It occurred to us that she did not wish to be seen. She pretended to be hanging out her wash; it was hung on both sides, so we knew she was trying to catch us walking the path which lay hidden beneath her freshly sodded lawn. Knowing this, we did not venture to take a step onto our path. We were happy taking the extra-long route of fifty yards to the shoe repair shop. She then called us over. This Lady wanted to reach an agreement with us. If we three boys would keep those disrespectful children of the neighborhood from trampling down and killing the nice lawn the good Lord had given to their pastor and his wife, then she would make us fresh chocolate chip cookies. These would be served with a cool glass of milk.

It was an arduous task. It took us years of cookie-eating and tall tales to get that path out of the public's memory. The three of us had to check in with his wife several times weekly to assure her we were on the job. She used to look at our hands and then send us off to wash before presenting us with a hot cookie sheet filled with cookies. She would lovingly tap our fingers, telling us to be careful; the cookies were too hot to be eaten. Still, her cookies must have tasted better after our tongues were heated because we always devoured them hot. She would stand over at the sink pretending to be making something for dinner while telling us about her Jesus.

Though we knew of her husband, we really didn't know him. Whenever we went, he was in the back of their home studying or was out visiting. Sometimes, he'd pretend to smell the cookies and come out to get one, and being polite, he would always call each of us by our names. She would be over by the sink, busying herself and looking out the garden window. Before letting us leave, she always told us she loved us rascals and prayed that someday we would come to know her Jesus. I think that Lady lived to introduce people to him. We'd be sitting on tall stools at the little counter island while she'd be over at the sink talking away about her Lord. She'd often tell us, "Now, Babies, don't you go listening to what some man tells you. You have got to read and study His Word yourselves." Often, she'd ask if we had read our bibles. If we said we had, she'd ask questions about where we had read. It did not matter where we read; Mama Porter could take any passage to talk about her Jesus.

Chapter 29

Sometimes, mumbled talk would find its way about town to fall upon my ears. It was simple to talk about new or better things which were coming. It may have been concerning a new park or a new store. It mainly happened when people believed it to be something good. When this happened, I used to listen to the people because the rumors came first, then the disclosure of where the talked about items would be located. They were predominantly placed on a property that some poor fool sold below market value to a wealthy land developer who had just purchased the property. Another tactic used to create wealth was to only allow a certain parcel of land to be developed. Still, this could only happen once it was purchased by one who was affluent or had supported those with proper political ties. I used to believe that if those fools had held out a little longer and had filled out the acceptable forms in an approved manner, they could have been set for life. I only understood why people cared so much about who purchased their land once I became painfully aware of the reason. I witnessed and overheard the small talk I titled the Country Clubs Corruption.

If the city received federal monies to improve the downtown's appearance, such as it was, it was not intended for everyone. This was brought to the forefront from the shadows when some properties along Main Street were outside a citywide improvement zone until a certain ex-partner of a particular politician obtained them. The two were rumored to be tight-knit ex-partners and a dangerous combination.

When I was younger, we took field trips in school. One of these outings was always to our town's library. The building our library was housed in was part of the estate a wealthy man left to the plebeian of the city. He was the man who controlled industry in his day. He owned the first brewery in the area. It was smaller than the one established by our so-called first president, but it was the best and most significant one in our town at that time. Some may not remember our first president was the wealthiest man in his state. He designed the grinding stone for his flower mill during the Revolutionary War. When he was not busy crossing the frozen river.

People worldwide desired his fine-ground white flour and sent their gold to obtain it. Often, during his war, he took a few moments to draft things for others to build. George lived what many consider to have been a charmed life. During all the battles he fought, while leading the charges and losing most of the actions, though his coat may have been torn by the enemy's shots, Gorge himself was never hit. I used to sit in that library trying to imagine why some seemed to live charmed lives. The man who once lived there was rumored to have lived such a life. His house was huge. It had an old grandfather clock imported from Germany on the right side of the main hall and a brick fishpond outside the courtyard. We smaller school kids read books around it. I used to go in the spring to try and see if the fish could survive the winter. Tales from older children floated down the stairs concerning how they caught some, once surviving the thawing process, and then they were able to free themselves from the last bit of ice to swim around as if nothing had happened. When I was a kid, I thought those goldfish lived forever, but whenever I bought one from five and dime, you could almost hear the flushing sound of the funeral.

The top floor of our old library was for lawyers only. I should have stated that it housed the local law library. This building was next to, though on opposing corners of our courthouse. The buildings were connected by a tunnel because lawyers couldn't be bothered by the imagined hoards who met outside the courthouse trying to meet them. When people wanted to meet our town's lawyers, they needed to make appointments or go to the bar off Market Street like the dolled-up ladies. They had to take a chance to find a lawyer who would play in public. Our library had a secret passageway that allowed lawyers to get to the law books unhindered. Some claimed it was an ideal setup.

When I flew back to attend my uncle's funeral, our library looked to have become private property. Some new low profile modern looking buildings, with only about half of it above ground a mile up Main Street, was the library. It was the site of the worst school building in town. That school was where summer school sessions were held. I could not help but question who made such an arrangement. How did the city sell a building which was owned by its plebeian?

There were a series of unsolved murders, which seldom affected the people of our communities. From time to time, along local truck routes, there were bodies discovered at the edge of town or a town nearby. It seemed always to be someone easily captured by the term of a poor, misguided stranger. They appeared to be about the same age. Their bodies would be naked and placed beside a tree, telephone pole, or road sign. What I remember is they all seemed to be good-looking. I also recall the people mumbling how they were probably just runaways as though such an explanation granted permission to accept their deaths. There must be a half dozen or so in our graveyard. These unmarked graves seemed acceptable since no one in town knew the girls. I don't believe there was much concern about the person who once housed those bodies. It seemed to appear the rush was to get through the paperwork and get them in the ground before people started counting or came to try and discover who they were. The last thing the powers that were needed was someone to advertise these murders. These victims' lives were reduced to brief obituaries in the local paper. No one seemed to mourn the world's loss or the promise of what might have been.

One of the younger queens used to come by to tell me dirty little limericks or jokes and began to visit my uncle's house. She did this embarrassing behavior against his son. She did not come to tease; she came to get a reaction that came with a captured prey whenever she exposed more than innuendos. She would wait for the right moment to reveal herself or tell her jokes and then laugh at the natural reaction. She lived to humiliate. The trouble with listening to her was you naturally begin to process the information. It had its effect: It wore you down. My uncle noticed something different about his son. He asked, and I answered. She stopped visiting.

Chapter 30

Thousands of faceless people have walked the streets of that city. Thousands have gone to work. They have driven cars through it, gone to school, and endured their existences. Thousands of faceless people were told and did what they were told, never questioning existence. I heard they simply accepted what they wanted to hear and walked around the time bomb, not knowing someone amongst us had struck the match. Their hands are or are said to have never reached out. They merely occupied space in that cold, calculating world that encourages its members to silently suffer through their existence.

I was working when a person from the state's Child Protection Agency called to ask questions. I have never liked talking with these people. They do not realize I have to relive the events to answer their questions. They come with questions, no none of them has answers. Her questioning was directed toward obtaining the conditions that produced her conclusion. Her conclusion was simple. He was guilty. She wanted to know what allowed him to commit these crimes against her state. The answer lay between thousands of unquestioned details. Details forgotten by those who study the hordes of those with a faceless existence whose silent screams warned, I realized that the tortured tomorrow we cried about was coming.

The person who called me from my past and I were talking. She'd read an article in the local papers concerning the crime. Forty-eight crimes were committed against the state. These crimes were forced upon a minor under ten. He swore that he had never intended to harm the soul of the child he sold. Clients were lured to him through the internet. One of his clients would testify against him. One was said to be from a respected family. As he sat, silently awaiting his fate. Some of the articles written were by those who suffered again when they read of his crimes. Some wrote of things they wished had happened as though they saw the facts, not the tortures released from a haunted mind. One article said additional charges from an adjacent county would be coming.

One claimed that when everything was said and done, the federal government would charge him with human trafficking. All these things were reported and then, all at once, hushed.

One of the victims talked. He did so to spare his new brother and sister. Their names were not being released. Sure, details were blocked from the public's view, but the young man should have been celebrated. The world should rise up and celebrate a child who sacrifices himself for the betterment of others. Still, he would become as forgotten as his acts of courage. He'll be reduced to a note in the memoirs of an agent's successful career. He will be brutalized by a system that claims it has rescued him. The state workers will look through the list of people who have come forward to raise the children on the back of society. The state determines who will care for these children. The children do not comprehend a system that claims these truths to be self-evident...All men are created equal and endowed by their Creator with certain unalienable rights. These children will become lost, searching for the meanings of the words only to discover these words do not apply to children. They will find the system does not know the importance of the word all. They would realize that all is only pleasant, society's interpretation of the word all.

People will rally about the cause, claiming they wish only to protect the children as thousands of other children fall beaten, hungry, and forgotten. The state will look through mountains of filed forms, giving the masses time to forget it was the state that declared the abuser was fit to raise the children. The state took them from the only existence they knew to place them under its protection. These children were removed from everything they knew and planted in a new culture with two families' offspring combined to become one family under the direct of a state-approved single parent. They traveled to their new house fifteen thousand miles from all they knew. Such is the treatment we give prisoners of war to thwart their desire to escape and add to their captures' ability to contain them. I also heard rumblings about his planning to move before his capture.

The voice of one I knew in the past read messages from people who posted on a website. She would tell bits and pieces about the family's acts; then I would describe to her how each family member would react.

I explained what their action brought to the forefront of my mind. People were writing the website demanding to know what was being done. Some recorded the brutality of words as though words were not weapons. People were expressing anger and demanding answers. Some were angry at the state, some voiced disgust at the system, and others at life and trying to find peace within themselves. Some I identified as past victims of the family. They were seizing the moment. They were checking to see if anyone was listening yet.

Crimes of the past resurfaced in their minds and lurked at their doors. Some mothers abandoned their children or used them as ponds to obtain their desires. There is the stepfather who peeped through windows. The man was infamous for the molestation of his nieces, nephews, daughters, and sons. The father exposed himself to young children at the mall. The granddaughter's husband had an affair with her mother before her. Then had one with the grandmother, after they had secured all the old girl had. The robbing of the elderly by her grandchild and various other crimes against the state. Still, these things were enacted upon individuals. Crimes committed by a person the children were demanded to trust and look up to. If one dares go to the authorities, they are told that the crimes are civil matters, and the cops didn't have time or the manpower to investigate the issues. These were maddening times due to the conflict between conscientiousness and the lure of existence.

As I was conversing with her, I questioned whether or not those who saw it were accountable for their versions. If it is true that all evil needs to prevail is for good men everywhere to do nothing, the answer must be, "Yes," they are accountable." The question, therefore, should become, "Is the cost of silence greater than the cost of their exposure?"

Chapter 31

When I became a teenager, my friends and I would drive to the creek to swim. This is the same creek I rode my bike to with a childhood friend. The swimming hole was a mile off the road but an easy hike through a cow pasture and a small, wooded area. When we were younger, we would celebrate our arrival by fishing for smallmouth bass; if this proved unsuccessful, we'd swim. We'd also swim whenever we grew bored with our success. Once, while we were there, the youngest of the newly crowned queen's husbands came. He tried to stir things up. I had all I needed and told the others I was ready to leave. He came over and, taking hold of my shoulder, spun me to try to boy me. I looked him in the eyes and said," I was raised in hell, and you're crazy if you think I don't know how to raise it." It was on. He swung at me. Even then, I knew there was no such thing as winning a fight, but I was the one who walked away after this one. While walking from the place, one of the guys with me asked who he was and why he had singled me out. I told him he was the latest to marry my cousin and felt I was in their way.

The truth is, we never escape our abuses. It doesn't matter if we get away; our memories hold the effects of the abuse. I understood the system was abusive, though some believe such abuses are to remain unknown. We, as most people, tend to stay with things that look familiar. We can walk away from the abuse, but we cannot hide our scars forever. We may choose to fight until we discover it to be another form of surrender. My solution was to be done. The others would no longer enter my decision-making process. I choose to endure, then leave them to their misery.

Before my phone rang with the advocate's call, I accepted the system viewed me as insignificant. I was a mere hurdle to another allusion to a successful career. If I had been maimed, disfigured by the acts the queen and her court had put upon me. If the state was found to be neglectful in any way to provide the proper protection, there would have been recourse. The state has the authority to intervene, but they are not accountable for intervention or the lack thereof. Power without accountability is a disastrous myth. I repeatedly told myself as a child, "The system doesn't care." Through their actions, they often proved me correct. Still, I never expected to meet someone in the system oblivious enough to tell me I was insignificant.

As the day of his trial slowly approached. Supposedly, how could someone for whom they demanded an answer be confirmed by an in-depth investigation? Things began to take shape. They wanted answers to all avenues they feared he and his lawyers might take them down. They made it clear they did not want any surprises to appear during his trial. They wanted the state's case to be open and shut. My sister said they asked if they could use her phone testimony in court. They didn't care much for what I told them. It appeared to be overlooked, but the person who broke the case was from another county.

Meanwhile, the local authorities assured the public they would delve into this tragedy's bottom. It is good that the leaders build their castles in the air, it makes it much easier to place foundations under them.

When I was younger, I knew bootleggers who conducted their business in the shadows of the old, covered bridge or way out on Horseshow Bend Road. Drugs were said to have been dispersed through the police department. Then, murders were not advertised; they were awarded back-alley dumpster cover-ups. Sometimes, those who were once behind the scenes surfaced to become pillars of the community. I wondered if they truly desired to solve the mystery behind the state's case. I knew there was a strong possibility some influential people might choose the chance to pass. *"All evil needs to prevail is for good men everywhere to do nothing.", My uncle has told me.* I understood some people would willingly supply a powerful reason to do nothing.

If the FBI were to search through our school's records, they should find where the case of a young lady had been dropped for an apology and admittance of guilt. The case was brushed aside to spare the school the embarrassment. Some of these hidden secrets were supposedly hidden before sending me through the school system. The girl's gym teacher liked to smell the armpits of braless girls after a brief conversation and accusation to prove the presents of deodorant after their shower. She was well known for demanding her students address her as she desired to be addressed. She pressed her proper title, Mss.

Because she had never married, she had a son much older than I was. To this day, it is hard to imagine her having a child. Not because she never married but because she was hateful. She looked like she could have been the model Picasso repeatedly painted, except she was monstrous. She ran over to me once during class because of the way I had addressed her. That teacher loved to tell us that our student handbook said we were to address as we wished to be addressed. I apologized while explaining I simply forgot she preferred Mss. Over Miss. I then explained that I chose Master over Mister. She had to call me master once before the entire class. It cured her of her imperial way. A few years after I graduated, a teacher from the system was sent to prison for practicing inappropriate acts with a minor. I often wonder why he was discovered; I know of another who did this and only had to agree to pay child support.

When I went to school, most boys took shop classes. I studied electricity, which had me going about the school, replacing lights and other minor things. I also took up welding, where we learned to stack beads. I took drafting and machine shop. During the half year I took Machine Shop, I finished the projects early, so I was permitted to work on my chosen projects. I decided to alter the screwdriver project. I made it more prominent and significantly increased its length. The handle was aluminum tapered away from my screwdriver's shaft for aesthetic purposes. The grip was knurled, and the taper was interrupted to allow milling, which created its square slot to place a wrench on to aid the breaking loose of the screw. I also fluted the shaft, where it went into the handle. When I took the components into the welding shop to form its blade and temper its tip. A heated bonding process ensured the handle would not slip on the shaft. I could turn them out every two weeks with lunch money and sell them to local farmers for thirty-five bucks. They claimed to need them to work on equipment.

My business was doing quite well until the shop teacher wanted his cut. The man thought he needed half. I did the work. I purchased the materials, found the customers, and established a clientele; the man wanted half. Even Hogs go hungry, is what the folks at the river said.

I simply choose not to make another. I did agree to pay other students to make them for me. I spent ten bucks on them. Sold them for forty-five because of material increases, not to mention supply and demand. This also was stopped once it was almost proven.

Shortly after this, I was approached by a couple of shop teachers. One guy taught minor engine repair, and the other taught automotive maintenance. I was told if I were to work with them on whatever projects they'd assigned, they would guarantee A's. Grades in that school system did not mean much. They tried to apply a little pressure, but I could climb anything I could get a fingernail on. That helped me to be seen as too valuable to my electronics class. That teacher had the most tenure. I did a little persuading of my own.

The teacher who taught minor engine repair had a nice thing going. People would come and drop off their bad motors, and he would swamp them out for motors that had been completely rebuilt. He'd rebuild it as a class demonstration if their engines were rare, valuable, or harder to work on. It ran like a smooth system where students received A's. Clients received suitable motors. The school had a seemingly endless supply of broken engines, and the teacher had a cash-and-carry success.

The Automotive teacher was part of an auto theft ring. He drove the cars to school for the students to fix. They got damaged while being taken. They would replace the broken window and repair the ignition. He'd have a few of his prized students detail them. All this was accomplished while charging it against the school's budget. When he could not explain the strange reoccurrences to a specific student's satisfaction, the student started counting the times he had to break into his cars because he'd forgotten the key. When the student discovered he carried a *Slim-Jim*, he lost his ability to believe the teacher and the law was notified. The rumor was these two were getting too big for themselves. It caused their fall from grace. It, and the fact they forgot they, also had to grease the wheels.

Chapter 32

A couple lived on the same hill as the man who controlled industry, but they were at the far end, near my grade school. As I walked, their house came before the mansions. It was an expensive though modest home in the best of locations. It had one of those meandering driveways cut into the hillside. It was painted barn red and had white trim. The gardener who took care of the mansions also took care of this lawn. People told us the man who lived there was the big-shot corporate lawyer. To be honest, I don't remember much about him, except kids all said he did not like kids in his yard. I didn't care; the sidewalk was on the other side of the street.

In the back of their home was a rolling, sweeping, tree-free hill perfect for the slaying. The mountain had a trickling stream that froze over and was great for jumping. People about town mumbled whenever they thought others weren't listening about why they couldn't have children. Some claimed it was because of breed. Others claimed it was because God knew who they were in the dark. Others said it was just some form of deranged punishment for something they had once done. Others claim those things just happen without rhyme or reason.

One day, when I was on break from the second grade, I was trying to ride my toboggan at school. I wasn't having much success because the bigger kids needed to give me a turn on the slope. I simply moved to an untried spot on the hill and gave it a test run. It went well, so I continued. With each run, the snow became tighter packed. With each packing came added speed. I was having fun and surviving the cold until I ran and hopped on that toboggan that last time. Now, a toboggan can only be guided, never steered. In the packed snow, the guiding was dismal at best. I nearly hit two large trees before I had to abandon my toboggan, allowing it to venture into the street. The Lady from the barn-colored house must have been watching because she came out of it so fast; she didn't even have her coat on correctly. She looked like she was scared; she also looked concerned. She looked like she had been through a disaster, not that she wasn't made upright, but that her face showed an underlying fear. Not knowing who I was, she started calling out to me by the title, "Little Boy, Little Boy." When I looked her way, she motioned me over. She asked me to follow her when I got as close to her as I dared. We began talking while pulling my toboggan up her drive, and she asked if I knew who she was.

I explained that she was the big-shot corporate lawyer's wife who didn't allow kids to play in his yard. The land became flatter when we came closer to their home, and I didn't need help. She asked me who I was, but I would only admit that my name was Jackson. Repeatedly, she asked whose boy I was, but I was not about to rat out myself. I knew she would have called mom, and I'd be in big trouble. Grandma would lie her way out again. I asked her if I had to tell her. She wanted to know why I asked. I told her I didn't realize the toboggan could do what it did. Then I explained how the big kids refused to give me my turn on the usual run. She asked if I wasn't ever going to slay down that hill again. I promised her I would not. She then asked why. I told the truth. I told her if she had not come for me, I would have pissed behind one of the trees already.

She looked at me and smiled. She tried not to laugh, but a little one escaped. We walked my toboggan over and placed it against their house. She led me into their home and pointed towards the hall where the bathroom was while giving directions. I was trapped in one of those snowsuits, mitten-gloved things (a hand-me-down from a cousin), and unable to see the zipper because of my hat and scarf. I looked like a wobbling red marshmallow, and I couldn't get my outer zipper down. She came to check on me and helped me out of the contraption.

I used their restroom, but she wasn't there when I came out to where I thought she'd be. I was in the second grade and had already been framed by some good-looking dame. Weekly, I called out, "Hey, Lady." She came quickly, probably because of the fear in my voice, then asked if I wanted some hot chocolate. We became instant friends. I was the only kid who could slay or toboggan down their back slope. She smiled when I came over. Sometimes, she stood by the window and clapped or waved when I happened to make it across the frozen stream by chance. I could go there and play all day, though she made me come into the house when my lips were blue. I'd go inside with her for a little while to warm up. We ate cookies and drank hot chocolate from a pan with a pouring lip. She used milk to make her hot chocolates. They were topped off with marshmallows or whipped cream.

She would ask questions about school and other things which ran through a child's mind. We ate sandwiches and chips for lunch. We could laugh at nothing. When she figured out who my mom was, she promised not to tell our secret. She thought it best if I told mom I played on their hill. I should not have listened. I got a lecture and my rules of behavior in their home. Mom told me she knew them. Said they were friendly people. I didn't get to know him, though he'd sometimes come home for lunch for some critical papers he had forgotten. That Lady loved me, and from her, I learned to look for the neck which turns the head. He may have been the big-shot corporate lawyer at the office, but that was her home, and I could play in her yard because she said so. I always had to go into their house to receive my treats on Halloween. She never pinched my cheeks, but she gave great hugs. I liked surprising her. She looked happy to see me whenever I came. Most people said they were a lovely couple. I only knew her.

When I was a kid, our little league took us to a Cincinnati Reds game once a year. We went to the old, old field. It had a hill in the outfield. This outfield stopped where the train's tracks cut through. I was at the game when their rookie catcher hit the homerun off the coke sign and collected what I recall to have been $500 extra dollars. We loved the Big Red

Machine. During the warmups, Pete Rose would come out in the outfield and tip his cap to me. Pete played the game the way its inventor imagined it should be. When I was a kid, Pete Rose was the man. I still like Pete, though we have never met. They used to call baseball America's game. I don't know why we allowed it to happen to the game. Some will never comprehend a man's effect on men. That commissioner and his trap. One man should never be permitted to be unchecked. I watched a show where this guy interviewed some players and asked if the commissioner should have gotten away with it. They him-hauled around, reminding me of the child's game I tried when I didn't wish to be caught. I would hold up an item of clothing and ask mom if the thing was clean. She never once looked at one. She'd just say no. She knew she'd have to wash it. It took me a while, but I figured out mom believed it couldn't have been clean if I couldn't tell. I wanted to understand why we allowed certain things to continue. We all should stand up and demand that America's game listen to America. Whenever justice is denied for one, it has been denied to all. The hall of fame is supposed to be about how the man played between the lines. It would be wrong to allow his name and player to be forgotten in Cooperstown. I know all about if he would have only...This is not about Pete; it's about Jackson and all the other kids that looked up to him. What have we done to deserve this punishment? I believe those naysayers would still be throwing stones unless Mama Porter's Jesus was there.

Chapter 33

A man worked at or owned a little market at the southwest edge of our neighborhood. This guy was well-known throughout high school. He had two well-loved sayings concerning a single topic. They were "If they are old enough to go die for this country, you're old enough to drink in it." and "Any man who's married is entitled to drink." High school kids would go in after turning their class rings over to make them look like wedding bands. They'd show him the back of their class ring, and he'd declare them married. High school students used to gather in little groups about his parking lot. That lot was twice as long as it was wide. It was not penetrated by the sidewalk like the other lots along the street. The parking lot did not have a single line or arrow to give directions. If you were to pull into that market, it was assumed you knew how to get what you wanted. It had a payphone about twenty feet from the face of the curb along the left side of the market as you faced it, but its light was never lit. This booth was beside an overgrown shrubbery mass, protected by four yellow-painted steel poles embedded in and filled with concrete. Sometimes, cops would drop by to have their coffee freshened up while waiting for their sandwiches. Sometimes, they came in to check on the upstairs.

Sometimes, the old man would leave the store to go out and talk with a group of the gathered kids in front of the ice cream ordering window. He would tell stories about his time in the Navy during the big one.

"When I was in the navy, the ships were wooden, and the men were steel." He had tattoos on both arms. One arm was a naked woman who was beginning to need a dress. It was a big thing to get him to flex his muscles and make the woman dance. He seemed to be expecting the cops to come by. I overheard him talking to a cop about some of the gathered guys. It was about who could be trusted to do a job correctly and keep their mouth shut. The man had a little market. In it, he sold bread, deli meats, canned goods, beer, soda, milk, a few baby supplies, and the best soft-serve ice cream in town. However, some claimed his occupation was scouting for the force.

Chapter 34

It is strange the things a mind remembers. I hear others talk of their past, and they can tell of their growing process in a straight line. I can't. When I get close to painful memories, I must back up and lay a foundation before exposing the memory. Not doing this would be an acceptance of the event. There are holes and jagged edges in my memory. When I try to smooth my memories, they become filled with lies. I struggle for clarity through truth, which can be seen in the mist.

I remember the earth's rebirth in vivid colors when all my senses were heightened during the floating cessation, which overwhelmed me following my passage through an acceptance of death. I became amazed by the prospects of life. I often fought for a chance to live, yet there were a few instances where I thought death was imminent, and I surrendered life's fight. I calmly accept death's grasp. I remember looking around and thinking, "This is how it ends." I was not afraid, nor was I welcoming death. I was sort of fascinated by the perceived ending to my existence. I remember the vivid colors fading to black as I was choked unconscious. I recall the surprise of awakening in the same world as the person who choked me cried uncontrollably, telling me she could not live without me. Within moments, she became unable to recall what she'd done. I remember laying down watching TV and being repeatedly kicked in my ribs and then pounced upon while being screamed at.

I don't know what I did, nor can she recall doing it. I remember lying there while she kicked away. I also recall the bruises and peeing blood for days.

There is no logical explanation. When I hear accounts of someone's violent upbringing, and the version flows smoothly, I believe they have been deceived or are lying. I think this because existing is filled with contradictions, and it dares us to venture outside logic's boundaries.

There was a ring of thieves who would rob stores or houses. They were never caught, to my memory, though they were very well known. These thieves didn't keep what they took. They took as they were instructed. It is said they learned from who they would take it. They stole anything from a box of gum to a car. They were never caught, and insurance companies paid regularly. The little market, which I believe was owned by the tattooed man, had a large warehouse connected to it in the back. Regular delivery trucks were never seen at those docks.

The market was a concrete block building on the bottom. Over its entry was a patio to the apartment which was above. To the left of the entrance and about fifteen feet in on its unpainted concrete floor were shelved items. To the right were racks filled with candies and the counter. The only thing on this counter was the day's newspaper, already read and wrinkled, a cash register, an open carton of beef jerky, and a display of *Timex* watches.

Dad purchased my first watch there when he figured I needed to learn to tell time or desired that I stop asking him what time it was. Cigarettes and the stores' cheap cigars would line the shelves behind this counter. Cartons of cigarettes were beneath this display. They were placed in this location to take advantage of the store's lighting and prevent thefts. The wrappers of the cigarettes cause the packages to dance in the light whenever they come out of someone's shadow, or the door opened. On the other side of the counter was the deli. You could purchase fresh, cold cuts or have someone make your sandwich.

Redwood siding was on the market's newer section of the lower portion. This part was where we went for soft-serve ice cream. You had to step up to the little window and ring the tap bell. You had to slap it repeatedly if you wanted someone to come. If you did this eventually, they would. They had to pass through a little room after passing through a smaller storage place that was connected to the store by its west-side wall. The bottom of the store was white. It was flat white and would leave a chalk mark on your clothes if you brushed against it. The apartment also had white wooden siding, though it had black shutters secured to the building for appearance's sake.

There was a small grass area kept inside a chain-link fence. This portion was gated to separate the apartment's entry from the parking lot. In this area, the concrete steps rose toward the tiny porch, which led to a narrow balcony granting access to the apartment or its green- (fake grass) carpeted patio. The concrete steps sat on I-beams that jutted out from the concrete blocks of the lower market and rested on a single but much larger I-beam. This beam ran from the concrete pad on the side of the grassy area to the balcony's little porch. One could see a small round metal table with chairs on the patio. The upstairs patio would protect its people from falling because of its black rod iron fence/railing. Halfway along the balcony was the apartment's red entry door. This apartment was lit up at night by the glow of a yellow bug light. I never witnessed anyone parting the sliding glass doors to come out on the patio. I can't even recall those curtains ever parting. What I remember is that the market was never robbed.

I lived near that market for the earliest years, and the place is a mystery. As a kid, I was almost afraid to look at its apartment. People would have to be crazy to steal from that place. Everyone said the old man kept a sawed-off shotgun beneath the counter. The cop's latest girlfriends seemed to always move in upstairs.

I was out of grade school before I realized the girls were changed periodically. The only time I saw the girls were when they stood behind the lace curtains of the picture window. As a kid, I tried to train my eyes not to look up. I never knew where these girls came from or where they went, for that matter. That big window filled most of the wall between the red door and the patio. When older, sometimes, I would spot one of these longing ladies looking past herself through the void to dream of the world that awaited her.

They remain haunting memories. I always saw these ladies as lonely, though certain people were said to have visited frequently. I can't recall seeing one girl ascending those concrete stairs or sitting on the covered patio. I lived by that place for years and never unraveled its secrets.

Dad used to take us to that market to purchase our candy on his Saturdays. I used to love those fresh, soft cherry licorice snakes.

Chapter 35

There was a wooded area outside of town. The site was haunted, if only in local superstitions. Few mentioned it above a whisper, and I don't recall anyone discussing it openly. Those woods looked much the same as all others in our area but were different. The river ran through them on its way to some other world. I fished the sides of the wooded area but have never desired to fish where the river cut through those woods. Nor did I venter to step foot on its banks. Everyone knew those woods were off-limits. If a car broke down while speeding through, cops would come to help the drivers. They would rather push people to safety and never leave them stranded. It wasn't the darkness they held to; nor the sounds they echoed. It was the fact that they were unsafe. Even when passing through during the daylight, I felt uneasy. Those woods made you feel like even the trees were spies. When I came to those woods, I stopped fishing and started paddling. When he was younger, one of the old river men who had become a down-and-outer claimed the man who owned the gravel pit had paid him to build a log cabin there. I never saw that cabin. I always looked for it as we drove past but never saw it. Nor did I see smoke rising from a chimney during the dead of winter. I did not like those woods, and after fall, when the trees lost their leaves, those woods never exposed their secrets.

I knew most of the woods around town. I'd gather mushrooms in the spring and hunt for rabbits, pheasant, and quail in the fall or winter. In return, I'd have to relieve the owners of their groundhogs, skunks, and the like. The farmers did not like groundhogs and would pay to get one. I knew the fields, farmers, and woods about town, but I never wanted to learn those superstitious woods.

I knew of a family who once lived in an old army tent. They lived in one of the other woods outside of town. Steam, which fed the river, supplied their water. Though the river is where they bathed. They were friendly people. They had a boy who was my age and one who was a year or so younger. Their mom would stay near their tent all the time. She'd busy herself tidying up and reading. The Dad was a rugged outdoor type of man. He operated heavy equipment.

The oldest son and I fought for the last time in seventh grade. I always believed no one won fights. You fought to defend your principles, though I cannot tell you what that fight was about. I didn't fight as a kid much. I never looked for a fight but never understood the value of walking away. I knew fighting was a losing proposition. Even dogs won't trap one another. Dogs leave an avenue of escape. The one that accepts that route does not wag its tail. It looks away from all the other dogs. Some people have claimed these dogs don't carry the scars or need time to heal like the dogs that fight. I've never been convinced of it.

What those dogs receive is an opportunity to walk. They can gather themselves in another place to try to live again. My physical wounds healed much faster than the mental scarring. I can walk down the street and be totally absent-minded about the gash in my thigh I received during the fourth-grade summer while escaping the house for an hour or two. I cannot, however, walk down the street and not see the lessons taught me by the abuses of my past. The lessons of our past are not suppressed; they are the building blocks of our lives. The Lawyer's wife, who made the best hot chocolate, taught me revenge was never the answer. She claimed, "For one to exist to punish others who have wronged them is to throw your opportunity to live away." "The best revenge," she'd claim, "is to live a good life. Strangely, life's most important decisions are made during a brief passing moment. That lady loved me, and I love her. She took the time to guild me, but more importantly, she treated me like I had value.

Chapter 36

We had a little bar outside of town, and it was out of the way to get to. They would not allow guys under twenty-one. Most bars like this had gravel parking lots with older, broken-down cars and trucks. Not this one. It had the most excellent vehicles. Fast ones, luxury ones, and a paved parking lot. You didn't see any family cars there. When men went to this bar, they drove their toys.

It was well known that the older married men of our community would go there to meet young single ladies who may or may not have been twenty-one. It was also agreed upon that these young ladies were not interested in finding a meaningful relationship; they were looking for a fun night on another's tab. They said people were amazed at the place when they first went in. I've been told there were no peanuts at their counter or pretzels on the tables. They served great food, and their bands were the best around. I've been told that the bands were backed by a well-equipped Jukebox during the week. When I was little, I used to think its sign read Bar & Girl, not Bar & Grill. I knew a few of the vehicles that parked in this lot. Their wives would ask them to swing by the house and pick up the laundry.

Our town had a house over in Hollywood. They claim they had some wild goings on in that house. It could not have been a nice of a place to look at. Usually, there were Cars parked all over the lawn.

Behind this house was a flood control channel where I never saw water. On the other side of the canal were the county fairground horse stables. Some people kept their horses there year-round. This gave them easy access to the track to train or exercise their horse. It was ideal for city people who dreamed of owning a racehorse. The smell after it rained was the only bad thing about this location. Still, they claimed the smell never affected the little houses' business.

There was an old farmhouse just on the other side of town. The woman who owned it allowed others to farm her land for half the profit when their crops came in. The ladies who worked in her place were said to have looked more sociable than those employed at the other little house, but they had the same jobs. I always thought it odd, but each house's clientele seemed to accept where they were to go.

The wealthy people of the town had chaperones or escorts when they had needs or desires. Strangely, people accept what others tell them about their life's station. People would preach to me not to get above my raising, then try to teach me, "We hold these truths to be self-evident." They could spout both sentences from the same throat and never question if the words flowed from the same source. Occasionally, there would be talk about how some lonely, wealthy soul fell in love and rescued one of the ladies from her terrible fate. I had never met one who'd been rescued. I never saw a single lady going in, come out. Those places were pits where men threw away money, and ladies went to surrender their souls. The lure of easy money seemed to linger, but its cost was never told.

Chapter 37

Among my first memories are those concerning people who are not in our family. They were people who happened to live near us. There was one lady who needed to be corrected a lot. I cannot recall why her level never came into plumb, but she had trouble connecting her thoughts with their probable outcome. Her husband was away at work, and she was alone with their baby. Money was tight for them, mainly because it seemed that way for everyone else. I remember this lady had crazy schemes or plans to save a buck. Anyway. One day, after she had given their baby its bath and put him down for a nap, she decided she would save money and wash up in the sink using his bathwater. I remember loving this lady. Even though she was a bit off-center, she was very good to us and would play with us as if we were her own.

That day, she called out to us. I had never seen an outside our family naked grown woman until her. She wasn't changing or posing; she was stuck in the sink. We tried to get her out, but she was stuck fast. We had to get mom. Mom yelled at us to stay out. I didn't know you couldn't see other women naked. Then the fire trucks came. They came in the big truck with the ladders, leaving the fire engine in the station for another call. One of the firemen was young. The older, more experienced firemen didn't permit him to go in. When she heard the truck come screaming down the road. We could hear her crying with their siren. The trucks' big red lights were flashing, so people left their homes to see what was happening. The old firemen came out with the strangest looks on their faces. I guessed it isn't every day firemen get to rescue women from the danger of being stuck in the kitchen sink forever.

My other memory involved my dead brother, two girls, and myself. These girls were friends. My brother played with the oldest girl, and the middle girl and I played together. I don't recall going through that "It's a girl!" phase in either direction. We always knew these girls. Our moms went to church together, and their dad and our dad were drinking buddies. The oldest girl and my brother were talking in the backfield where the squirrel had caught my brother.

Naturally, being the younger brother, I wanted to get in on whatever they were doing. When I asked, my brother said they were playing house, and I'd need to become a couple if I wanted to play. I asked the middle daughter to marry me. That ended their game, but did he have fun teasing me. Mom must have been looking out the window and figured something was wrong. She called us. We had to go in. She finally got out of me what happened. Without skipping a beat, she looked at me and told me not to worry about their thoughts. Mom told me she thought she was a lovely girl and would someday make some lucky guy a fine wife. Mom was not talking down to me like a lot of adults did. She was talking to me about life while I was a child. When my brother thought he could get away with a secret teasing of me about my proposal, I looked at him. I told him mom approved of my choice of women and said it was alright for men to like women. I learned if the teasing doesn't bother you, it very well can irritate others.

Chapter 38

We had a different type of family in our neighborhood. The parents were already old. They looked more like grandparents with their grey hair and furrowed skin. They wore old people's clothes. Still, the kids were somewhat regular. The oldest son was a famous rock musician. At least he was celebrated in our neighborhood. He did live in New York, and the band he was in did have hit records. Many of the ones he plays with are famous around the world. We could hear their playing coming to us over the New York radio waves. Some band members were black. When he'd bring them to his parent's house, we would listen to them jam and play basketball in the alley. They were good guys, not much in the way of playing basketball, but good guys.

In the house, the old couple had silver serving trays complete down to the sugar bowl, salt and pepper shakers even the pickle dish. Those aged parents sat around their bricked-off fireplace in big flower printed wing back chairs to read old people's books. When they heard us coming through their basement, they would put down their books to pick up their teacups or a little plate of cookies. Those cookies were terrible. They would only nibble on those things after soaking them in tea or coffee.

A lot of the other parents talked about these two. Some never liked that she kept the nice car. A newer *Continental* while he drove about in a heap. His car was the remains of a brown paper bag-colored Plymouth station wagon. It smoked, backfired, chugged around turns, and hummed itself to stops. When he turned, it would lean. It had no remaining floorboards in the back seat, so you could dispose of the drink if the cops pulled you over. He used that thing as a truck even though it was the barebones remains of what was once a family car. It had survived several non-garaged eastern winters. Teens used to pop the hood to put those things on the coil wire, which causes a car to smoke more while it chugs and whistles. Sometimes, that old thing would just stop and chug and whistle; after the pop, it would run again.

Most of the complaints about those old parents were about them being elitist. They were distant, ancient, and tight. Their dad paid me twenty-five cents for scrapping paint off their Victorian-style home. He then acted insulted when I refused to do his stinking garage. They raked their backyard leaves into a vast pile, then put them in sheets to try and sneak them over our back fence to dispose of. I had to walk out and talk to him that day. I tried my best not to let on that I knew his purpose for being out behind our garden. I asked him if he had read any good books lately.

They were a strange couple. If he owned an item, it was priceless; if he wanted your thing, it was a piece of junk he was willing to take off your hands. They held to that criminal mentality where the wrong they'd committed was always someone else's fault. He was an insurance man by trade, but listening to him talk, I discovered every sale had its scam.

They tended to put on as though they did not belong in our neighborhood, but the kids never seemed to have caught the disease. They skipped school, hopped on the trains, and did as we did. Watching when one of their boys got into trouble at school was great. He would come out of his broken-down wreck, which once resembled a car, but only to readjust his clothes. Then, he would straighten himself up to his full height. The man had to stoop to pass through doorways. He would march into the office indignant, demanding to know who had dared to question his child. He looked willing to scratch, bite, or claw anyone who would defy him while swearing that his child would never have done such a thing. His deep base voice would let them know the school had to be mistaken because he and his wife gave their children a proper upbringing.

That man could rant with the best of men. When he got going, a little white pasty-looking dot would form on the center of his top lip. As a child, I knew when this happened to stand back and question him. Finally, that dot would fly off when he had to pronounce a p, and the man would crumble under the embarrassment of spitting. It was a game we played to relieve the pressure of being scolded. Say what you will; the man could get us out of trouble with the school if his kid was thought to have been involved. After being freed from the school, we had to wait for the dot to appear. Once it was launched, we were left to correct ourselves.

Chapter 39

Our school took us on field trips when I entered the third grade. One was to the zoo, and the other was to the art museum. We went to two of our state's most significant cities back-to-back. I liked the zoo. I liked seeing the animals I had only heard about and seen in print before the journey. I was also fascinated with the people. However, when we walked into the museum, I was amazed. The one-dimensional drawing and painting did little for me and could not hold my interest very long. However, when we entered the room filled with Impressionist, I was blown away. I loved the museum. To become absorbed in the work of someone who came before... to behold the beauty they found and captured for me to discover.

Museums were great gentle reminders for those who had lived. They were encouraging me to strive for life. I recall studying the paintings. When I got close, there were dots, splashes, and slashes from the artist. When I removed myself from their space, they became photos. I still recall liking one of a lady sitting at a rod iron table near a stream by a bridge. Small splashes of color depict a scene from life. I understood the lady posed. I knew most of the view had been arranged. Close up, the thing was not much more than a blur. However, given its space, its beauty began to unfold. They were great depictions of life.

Chapter 40

Life throws us curves. The Sunday my brother died, I decided to slip off and go to the river. I was below the dam, casting off the bank into a hot spot. I was slaughtering smallmouth bass on night crawlers. Something did not seem right. There was a cloudburst, and it began to pour. Somehow, I knew I had to get to the house. I cannot explain it. I knew where I had to go. As I was preparing to leave, I looked downstream toward where I thought I heard a low-flying car leaving town. As I did so, I looked toward where my brother had died. I heard the crash. The rain left as quickly as it came. It wasn't a thunderstorm. As I looked in the direction from where I heard the car, something happened. It was like someone dimmed the light on one of those multiple staged lamps. All during the storm, the sun stayed out.

When I got to our drive, I turned in and threw that bike to the ground. I was outside the garage pulling off my boots when a lesser queen slammed her powder blue Chevy Corvair into the driveway. She ran from the car and into the house. A cop car soon followed. I was laughing to myself, thinking she would finally be arrested. I went in to watch them cuff her and cart her off.

The cops had mistakenly gone to her daughter's place and told them my brother had been killed in a crash. My oldest sister called the church, telling them to tell mom to get to the house. I heard her say to the church's greater to send mom back to the house, then state she did not have time to explain. We stood about the place in disbelief, waiting for her return. I went outside. When my mother got out of her car, the cop riding shotgun stepped halfway from their cruiser and said, "Your boy is dead."

He did not even get completely out of the car. He did not allow her to sit down or go in the house. He had a message to deliver; he delivered it and tried to get back in the car. I charged him.

He did not tell her which of her boys had died.

Mom's scream was so loud and painful faceless people appeared from all over our neighborhood. As she screamed, she fainted. Her head hit the drive hard enough to free the hair from her bun. I was prevented, but I tried to get to that cop. I can picture him to this day. He was slender, stood about five-ten, and would have weighed around one hundred and fifty-five pounds. The cop had no visible marking to be used to identify him, and he wore no viewable jewelry. His hair was a dark brown, which could easily be mistaken for black. The irises of his eyes were two shades of brown. At first, they appeared to be a light brown, but as I drew nearer, they had streaks of a dark brown shooting from them like the spokes of a wheel.

His eyes opened wide as I went for him. His shoestrings were the thin, stiff, waxy type and were coming untied on his foot on the curb, as those often do. That man's words and image haunt me to this day.

That, and the fact the house allowed my hateful queen aunt to go and identify my brother's body. My sister and great-uncle went to inform dad. Our pastor came over to offer support and comfort the best he could. My sister and great-uncle returned, saying they could not find dad. I told my fixit uncle if he'd drive, I'd tell him. Dad came into the first place we went, "The Ice House," as we pulled out. I had to tell dad his name's sake had been killed in a car crash. I then invited him to the house. He was explaining that he would not be welcomed. Still, my fixit uncle assured him it would be alright under the circumstances and stated it would probably be best if he'd come. Shortly after our return, dad knocked on the house's door, which had never welcomed him. I looked about, knowing the house was aware of his coming. I introduced him to our pastor. I watched the faces of those familiar family strangers. They ignored dad as he sat in a small wooden chair in the corner between the kitchen and living room like some schoolboy in trouble. Mom's family was walking by him. Not one of them spoke.

The house refused to acknowledge his presence or the loss he must have felt. None of us were asked our opinion concerning my brother's final services. This decision was made by the Queen and her court.

Never again did I willingly take trash from any of those people. If you were to ask them, they would tell you I was mean and crazy. What I was... I was through. It was there, at that site, at the treatment my father received. I determined that the house would not stand for me, therefore, I would stand for myself.

At the viewing, my brother's body was the first corps I ever saw up close. I met some of dad's family. Others from his family came also. I was told I had met them before, but I would have been too little to remember. My brother's body looked swollen. There wasn't a mark except for a little cut slightly above his right eyebrow. His hair was slicked back and not parted in the middle. This was to help hide the hole in the top of his head. People were saying it looked just like him, but I knew they had his look wrong. Those making those comments only showed their lack of knowledge concerning us. I knew the coffin held a body, but that thing lying there was not my brother.

Most of the other scenes concerning the funeral are surreal. I was out of it. I sometimes think they drugged me to keep me silent. I remember wondering how those people could eat. I remember watching them gorge themselves from a safe distance. I remember thinking the house was not concerned with what it permitted our ears to hear. I remember the queens looking through and taking the food the people brought. Mom went to pick out his casket with our oldest sister, and they purchased a vault. I could not leave his graveside. I kept thinking, imagining strangers throwing dirt on that thing I was now to call my brother.

A little while later, before my dad died, I saw the lady who kicked me off her property because my dad drank. She came to me not knowing how to apologize and needing some noncommittal small talk. There was some mumbling of her son being in senseless trouble. She asked if I had any idea where she might have gone wrong.

I believed a lie. I thought vengeance would be sweet and better served cold. I opened my throat, parted my lips, and formed these words, "Perhaps you should have married the town drunk." Those words were brutal and cut through her sharper than any surgeon's scalpel could. The horror that reformed her face said more than words could ever express. Vengeance is not sweet. Vengeance is a gnawing that sours the depth of my stomach. It's a memory of cruelty that I cannot escape.

I never saw dad alive again after he came to the house when my brother died. Shortly afterward, he relapsed and was taken back to the hospital. When his employer's insurance ran out, he was taken to the big city and placed in the VA hospital. He was never released. I was dad's only legal heir because of the VA's interpretation of the divorce settlement. No one would take me to see my dad. He was forced to die alone. When the Navy checks came in my name. I was warned to sign them over to mom or else. These were large check payments because his ship was sunk at the end of WWII, and he should have received 100% disability but received 0. My mom and my oldest sister took care of most of the paperwork. They did so as though no one else had a say.

My oldest sister gave away all his vehicles even though dad left them to me. She gave them to some jerk for his work at dad's place. Gave my pieces of dad away for less than five hundred dollars worth of work.

That jerk came by the pool and bragged about the cars and an old Model A pickup he'd gotten from some stupid girl. No one was looking out for me. I stumbled through an existence where I learned to pick myself up, dust myself off, and try to move on. It was accepted; the house had done enough. It robbed me of my inheritance to give to others.

In that period, just a few days after my brother's funeral, the reinstated Queen delivered that magical baby. He came to live at the house. This is not unusual because grandma took his mother home with her. Giving the house the magical baby gave two additional queens the right of passage. Thus, the house's entrapment began. I was starting to be accused of instigating things whenever I stood up to a queen. When I started to defend myself, sometimes, they would switch punishments and try to have a battle of wits. That was fun but a little like a shootout against an unarmed man. They had declared me a fool who would never amount to anything. Therefore, I had nothing to lose. If they perceived they had won a battle, no bows could be taken; they had merely outwitted a fool. However, when they lost, it was humorous. Once they realized they could not be correct, they'd decide that the winner would be the loudest. They had nothing to gain from their little tirades. I was trying to understand why they wished to continue. They had taken control of the house, and no one wanted to be outsmarted by a fool.

Still, they would come to taunt me. I existed, so they went to great lengths to humiliate me before the others. I began giving them things to think about. Still, I had been sentenced. Sentenced to be a stranger in the house. The common enemy of queens. They would hold up the magical baby and be granted the right to fulfill their heart's desire. Food was redesigned for their use. Our money was taken at will and given to provide for their whims. They controlled the magical baby and, through manipulating him, owned the house. The house subconsciously would groan, fearing the loss of the magical baby. The magical baby was a mere pawn to be dangled and discarded so the queens could fulfill their every desire. The Queen and the magical baby's mother robbed us in exchange for the house keeping the magic baby. All that the queens did not steal was wolfishly accepted. Still, through it all, I stood as I warned I would. I was willing to suffer the cost of standing. The day of my escape was the Mother's Day that took my brother's life: the hour was when the house refused my father entry.

END OF PART ONE

PART TWO

Chapter 41

When I was starting out, I had a few strikes against me. My Dad was dead, and I did not have anyone. I had no family to speak of. I was alone trying to get my start. I did whatever I could to make a buck legally. An old couple I knew asked if I would paint their house. They needed new shingles, and two mulberry trees had to be made stumps.

I took the work. I cut those trees down. They were about two feet wide, but one was between the house and the garage. This called on me to lower it as I sectioned it out. I did this with a hand saw and an old double-headed ax. We removed the stumps by creating fire pits around them. I was just finishing the roof when a nice car pulled in front of their house. One of the guys acted like he was trying to intimidate me. The other guy wanted to help and teach me how to negotiate a better deal. I was told I was working in their area and that further work would only be done with their approval. The one guy asked what I was doing and how much I was making. I lied. I complained, stating they were my aunt and uncle, and mom was teaching me some sick lesson on responsibility before I had to return to school. They bought the tail, and I knew not to flash the cash.

The word got around about my willingness to work. Farmers called me to help bail hay or straw and other such chores. We bailed the old wire bails, not those light twin ones. Then, I was contacted by people who said there was money to be made in town, but I needed to be willing to grease the wheels. I'd been told several times about the squeaky wheel getting the grease, but in my town, the silent, invisible man behind the scene did not suffer. It was not so much the wealthy or the owners of our businesses that took advantage of craftsmen. It was the bankers/ money lenders and real estate brokers. They assumed none of the risks but demanded a big part of the profits for their helping you find work. They claimed they were helping you, yet your wage was predetermined before you arrived. The man who did the hiring and firing was just a shadow who had earned the right to rob you because of his loyalty to them. Whatever these thieves took from you was divided amongst themselves. You could try to refuse to play their game for a while, but hunger becomes a mighty motivator. The reality hits hard when you see the man drive away in his new truck, purchased through the profits you earned. To complain was useless. They had their positions, controlled the hiring and firing in the area, and knew their mirror images in the neighboring communities well. They managed all pay for those who provided a service. These men gladly supplied for themselves or encouraged poverty for those who remained outside their game. There was no flying below their radar. I was a kid learning I wanted to drive and trying to learn the nature of business. If you needed a job, you needed to know somebody. That somebody you needed to know demanded to be paid. He simply chose to withhold from you if you decided to withhold from him.

Chapter 42

I stayed near the river as soon as I was old enough
to get away with it. I loved the freedom of the river.
The city put a dam across it so people could water ski,
but the river still flowed. It still delivered its gift of life
to the fields below. In the spring, when the rains
came, the shallow streams that fed the river became
swollen, creating little pools of water for fish to live in.
When the river's edge returned to the silt, its
overflowing nourished the crops. I liked the river if,
for no other reason than no matter what people did to
it, it remained the river. Come winter, once its surface
froze, we would clear some snow off her. This area
was two blocks above the dam. We would dawn our
skates and play out in the open if we were inviting the
cops to come out and act like they wanted to run us
off. We skated under the bridge when we wished to be
left alone. If we were out in the open, the cops would
give us instructions based on the ice thickness. They
would stay to monitor us and drill holes to check the
ice thickness. Sometimes, they'd venture out on the
ice with their street shoes. It was fun playing keep
away. Sometimes, we'd pretend we couldn't hear
them. They would come out slipping and sliding like
they couldn't catch us. We really knew how to get each
other going. It would look like a scene from one of
those old silent movies. We could skate circles around
them, but they made it clear when they weren't
playing. Two of the guys I skated with as a kid became

professional scatters. When they returned to town, they told us that skating was no longer fun for them.

Through it all, I loved the river. I could lose myself fishing it banks from early spring to late fall. I caught bass in the morning and catfish after dark. Most people I met at the river were good people. They didn't hide behind their words. People on the river tended to say what they meant. If someone on the river told you to do right, it did not mean the same as if a city person told you to do right. Words seemed to be purer on the banks of that muddy river. In town, to do right meant to do what was best for you as an individual. In that instance, doing right needed to be justified. At the river, doing right told what was suitable for mankind. River-right could be considered city wrong because doing river right sometimes causes an individual to sacrifice. It might be that someone besides you still needed to catch their supper or what they needed to feed their family. This might have meant their kids would stay hungry. River right might call upon one to walk back from her banks without a fish but with a smile on their face. That is river-right. No justification was needed.

There were people across the river, below the dam, who worked at the paper factory who would talk down about the people who followed the river's flow. These people claimed if the river people did not have the river, they would not have sense enough to know how to eat. Those people had friendly offices, nice cars, and fancy homes. The river people questioned the prices they paid for them. People along the river were quick to help each other.

In contrast, those businesspeople seemed to view their fellow man as competition or prey. They claimed they had gotten ahead by climbing over the competition. I studied people, those along the river and those at the factory. Living in a kingdom can only be viewed as right when one sees themselves as the king.

The people who once cried for change did not want change. They wished only to exchange places with the ones who once caused them to demand change. Language is a miserable means of communication. Though some choose to look down upon us, the river flows; no matter what men do, the river flows. It was the flow of its muddy waters that taught me that we pay for the choices we make. There are yet two types of intelligence. There is river smart and city-wise. When you find yourself in a conversation, it is pertinent that you determine which language is being used to make sure the meaning of the words is clear. Words are a miserable means of communication. So much depends on the other's proper interpretation.

As one traveled out of town on the second of our major roads, a little past a soft serve ice cream shop, though it was on the other side, there was a beautiful piece of property. It was complete with rolling hills, a flowing stream, and about four hundred acres after subtracting wooded land and the pastures for horses and cattle. It was said to be some of the most expensive lands in our state. There was a mansion that sat upon a little knoll. This property was surrounded by an ornate cast iron fence around its picture-perfect established lawn and carriage drive. I had heard on several occasions the mansion was furnished entirely, but its treasures were hidden under covers. No one lived in this house while I was in town. No livestock grazing in its field, though one could see the pastures were connected to barns, with one set up for cattle and the other for horses. Even in its dilapidated condition, it was a beautiful piece of real estate. People around town would sometimes talk about it and tell of the deals they had once tried or tried to make with the old lady who owned the property.

The property was owned by the withering, bitter lady who owned most of the large old homes converted into multifamily dwellings on the wrong side of town. This woman brought mom a rag to mend to take a pattern from so she could have something to wear. She was an odd old thing... What I believed from all I was told is that when she was younger, she was beautiful and had a promising life ahead of her. She had studied music at the finest universities. After finishing her education, she went to New York to be discovered. At least, that was her plan until she met her husband. Some claimed she was once an accomplished concert pianist. Some in town claimed the old girl had lost reality, as happens when two people fall hopelessly and madly in love. They married, and he carried her back to his estate. They lived what many believed to be a charmed life together. They traveled as the wealthy do. They had a daughter. Her husband had converted their attic into a music studio so she could practice her entertaining at their social events to ensure their success. He was said to have bought, or perhaps I should state, he accrued properties about town. After they took possession of an old home, they were converted into two or three apartments.

Nothing wrong ever seemed to happen to them.

They were the toast of the town, and she graciously accepted being the bell of the social balls until one morning. He went out to do whatever he thought he needed that day and fell stone-cold dead. They said a blood vessel burst in his head, and he was gone before he hit the ground. Their daughter was trendy at school, as most multimillionaire pretty girls are. Her mother had buried her father when she met her daughter's beau. People claimed he was a nice guy. They also say he did not come from the proper social class. He was not from a poor family by any means. His family wasn't quite well off, and they earned their riches in a manner that would be hard to hide from those who flaunt their social graces.

This little girl had gotten everything she had wanted from her dotting father, who preached if she wished to do something wrong enough, she would find the way to obtain it. She received a new *Mercedes* for passing her driving test. She was what everyone said was the catch of the town. Yet, she was unavailable. She had accepted what her Dad told her. Her mother gave in and purchased that beautiful property. She paid to have it furnished as it was called to be. The garage had a brand-new custom-built brown *Mercedes,* for this child did not appreciate a caddy like her mother. Then, there were horses and cattle to be seen in its pastures. The problem was her mother could not bring herself to respect her daughter's choice of men. Since the daughter was very well off, she never accepted her mother's wedding present. She told her she would not until her mother apologized to her husband. That day never came, and the house remained unoccupied. Some about town claimed the old girl lost her grasp on reality when her child died. Others, such as myself, silently studied the river, knowing it had merely been exchanged. She began to smoke her cigarettes on long sticks. She would call boys to her caddy, pretending she needed their directions. I can't recall any boy who ever made that trip twice. "The old girl," they'd claimed, "had lost it." The rumor was she had never sworn she should have had a brilliant career. I believe she was once starving when her husband found her. He took her out and showed her a good time, and she began to imagine she had discovered the man of her dreams. When that little fish left her big city, she came with him. In our little city, she was the big fish. Then her dream fell, and her daughter went. Something inside her snapped. No longer could her playing be heard when walking by her mansion. No longer were the society people invited to dine at her table. No longer did she perform before the social elite. Something definitely changed. Boys would turn from her car with the strangest stories, though none would ever tell what they saw after running away.

Chapter 43

After my queen aunt had captured the third or fourth husband of her own. During the end of her present marriage, her soon-to-be ex-husband would come to the house for lunch while going through the divorce. Daily, but only on weekdays. That man could eat his weight in fried potatoes but never had a problem with whatever meat grandma put with it. He would only come for three-quarters of an hour. I remember these times well because we were locked out whenever he arrived.

Sometimes, his wife, a queen, would show up at the house the following morning. Her hair would be all lopsided and strands all hanging out. It always amazed me how those loose hairs emerged from that beehive, for the others did not move. I saw her put on hairspray; it looked like the bathroom had fog after she finished. Whenever she'd come over during the morning like that, she seemed to whimper; she was tired and needed a little bite to eat before going to her place to catch a little nap. She said she just stopped by to see what we had to nibble on while her droopy eyes could barely open. The whites of her eyes were yellow with red veins popping, and her nose was big and purple with holes all over it, but it didn't show the veins as her eyes did. She'd come in with her smeared war paint, but only because she needed something to nibble on. Grandma would get out of her chair and fix her toast, eggs, bacon, or ham steak, and I would be told to keep her company. As soon as grandma was out of sight, she would perk up and start bragging about the time she had the night before. If that woman was not bragging about it, then she was complaining about the one she did with the inability to do it right. During this period, the mean queen taught me how to pray. I prayed to God what she was telling me she and those guys did the night before was not valid.

When the strange man next door who looked over us moved into a split-level home he'd bought in the country, another couple with three girls moved in. His dad was wealthy, and his family appeared too proud to fit into our neighborhood. She owned some little yipping white toy poodle. That yipping mutt came to do its business in our yard meant I had to clean its mess. When I approached her, she asked me what type of person I thought she was, but I knew people who asked that question didn't really want the question answered. After having enough of her superiority, I took an old weed zapper. I coiled its wire around the bushes at the corner of the house where their yapper did its business. When she let Pheephee out, he damn near killed himself. The sound that the poodle made was not a yelp. When I got there, she was running to her precious poodle. It was still smoking. After that, the thing wouldn't put a paw in our yard if you called to it with T bones around your neck. I have never been one who liked that superior attitude. I figured out young that if those people are so unique, they must take their individual selves down the road.

When my queen aunt was younger, they said she fell in love once. They claimed she would have done anything for the man. According to those rumors, he was her world until she became pregnant. Then he wouldn't have a thing to do with her. Then, her husband returned from the war and found her pushing another man's baby in her stroller. Her husband demanded a divorce. The family would tell of these things to prove some people use you up and then throw you away. It was hard on her after her man refused to leave his wife and kids. They said he was a nice guy. Said he was some big shot in town. He was said to be a real high society man. They said she was never the same. "Love," they'd claim, "can cause people to do some strange thing." All I knew was she was mean.

She would do things to people in our extended family, which was unbelievable. She tried something with me, but I confronted her. She sent someone to correct me. That man did not appreciate my hard-headedness. She'd had lied behind my back. The woman lived to stir up trouble but steered clear of me. My uncle laughed, or perhaps a cackle broke through his grin. He said, "That, my boy, is why blue jays don't stir an eagle's nest." It took me a while, but I figured he knew she was mean, not crazy.

When I was a kid, there was a man who people about our town called the collector. I always needed to determine exactly who he worked for. He could be seen most days walking our streets. I would like to know if I ever heard his real name, but people knew him as Tommy the Taxman. People's faces told whether or not the person figured out who his employer was. Sometimes, when people thought they needed quick cash and were willing to pay, there were places they could go to acquire a loan. Though, these come at an unreasonable interest rate. There was more than one of these lending institutions. They seemed to employ Tommy. Tommy seldom spoke and never so needlessly. The talking was through if Tommy was sent to you for all practical purposes. Tommy came to collect things; TVs, recording equipment, your wife's wedding gifts, and other expensive items.

Most people feared Tommy. Everyone sensed what he did as he passed through with both hands in the oversized pockets of his trench coat. Even in summer, Tommy wore his overcoat. His hair was always in place. He wore a single jelly curl like he was about to perform in one of those old dew-wop groups. When Tommy came to visit, others sang. He had a long, skinny knife, which he kept in his coat pocket. His knife had a button that needed to be slid up to release its blade. Tommy kept his knife nice. I repeatedly heard that he was always packing but only pulled the gun if he intended to use it. He did not smoke and very seldom drank. Mostly, Tommy kept to himself. I never figured out where he lived. He would just say, "Drop me off here," then tell me I should be getting along. Those things which Tommy collected seemed to fail to work. He would trough them from a window and bounce them off the walls. The items

Tommy came to collect were often cleaned up and thrown out after being bathed in tears. The other thing is Tommy only came to collect once; if he came, the second time it was not for collection.

Tommy was a generous man. His teeth were long, skinny, and sharp. His skin was clean and caramel colored, but his eye looked into a void. He did not have a scar or blemish. People said Tommy gave broken bones and slashes with his knife, which ran curved, deep, and continuous. When I was younger, I walked behind Tommy through the worst parts of town. When I walked behind Tommy, no one bothered me. I felt the people grow nervous when they saw Tommy, but Tommy slowly walked through the town. When I was older, I gave him a ride. He was out in the country walking from those woods, which were different. I pulled over when I spotted him. He studied me and then got in. I asked where he was headed. He gave me a general idea. When he saw me, he never waved, committed himself to a smile, or did anything to acknowledge I was anyone he knew. After a ride, he said someday he'd be able to remember me.

I cannot recall the first time I saw Tommy, but I remember the first time Tommy saw me. Some kids and I from our neighborhood were out playing hide-and-seek. I spotted some kids hiding in the bushes and yelled something to help flush them. At that time, Tommy was passing through, and apparently, he thought I was yelling at him.

He turned to face me to let me feel the discomfort of being targeted by his eyes. I did not say a word; I froze in space until Tommy started to walk toward me. I started yelling that I had not been talking about him. I cried for the other kids to come from their hiding places. Once they came out, he allowed a grin to almost trickle out to his face. I was allowed to relax and breathe normally again. Tommy did not make a sound; he simply readjusted his steps to get back on his previous mission and quietly walked away. Tales concerning Tommy the Taxman were well known in our part of town. There, he was more infamous than famous.

Whenever Tommy was sent to a person, they were on time they had been paid for. When I was a kid, sometimes, people just came up missing. There were no bodies found. The odd thing was their wives didn't complain or go out to search for them. People knew what happened like they were missing, not missed. Worse than this, people seemed to understand and accept it as fact. A few of these guys had come back from being missing, however. They were permitted to maintain the appearance of a specific lifestyle. These would secretly tell a tale of how difficult it was to save your face once Tommy had come to declare you as missing. They would tell how his first ruling was to remove all doubt about who was in charge. They'd tell when Tommy came for that second visit, it was to confirm their new ownership. They all swore there were no terms. You were owned, or you went missing.

Tommy and I never hung out together. However, I did silently walk beside him through rough sections of town. I did give him rides, but picking up people you knew is what we did then. Tommy was never a friend; he was someone I recognized. I never felt like you should pass up anyone you could help, knowing I had been the one needing help and fearing I would be in that position again.

The last time I saw Tommy was right before he died. I was at the river when he came to me. From all he said, I thought it must have been hard for him to realize what he'd become. Tommy was a grown man who walked about our town like a leper. No one that I know ever communicated with Tommy. From what I saw, Tommy couldn't talk with anyone. His profession called for a certain lack of understanding and silence, mostly silence. I can't recall anyone ever asking about him. He was someone no one looked at whenever he came around on his assignments. Tommy was a silent taxman. As I grew older, I believed the town's underground loan provider was his employer. I suspect there was a head to the crime and that the person lived a life of luxury. I never bought into the theory about those down-and-out criminals. I knew some petty criminals, but even these thugs were soon introduced to the fact that our town had more than one force policing it. They were recruited if their talents were desirable; if not, they were dismissed. The head man could not afford to allow some smock going about his town haphazardly ripping off his clients or prey. I suspect all the underground loan providers were men who were once permitted to save face.

That time when Tommy came to me, he did not sneak over. He came in a manner that allowed me to know he was coming. It is the only time I remember seeing Tommy out after drinking. He must have downed a lot. Tommy was talking crazy about things that took time to make sense. He told me he'd understand if I thought his words came from his stupor. Tommy told me he went to college. Said he studied to be a doctor and had a remarkable life. Tommy had a wife and two kids. He described how one of his children was born sickly and knew the boy would never be right. He said he could never get overtaking his boy out in public and see good people looking at him and his boy like they were some freaks. He told me (Tommy His boy) had died. Said there was nothing anyone could have done. His condition first weakened and then distorted his body. The final stage of his illness was death. He told how his son had a sound mind and how they would talk whenever they went out, and the staring people started to wear on them. He said his son could understand the disease, but he never understood those wide-eyed people. For a while, I thought he was going to repeat himself. "You will never know the pain of going into a restaurant and seeing strangers staring at your son like he is some freak. "He told me while hanging his head. He spoke of his wife while slowly allowing his head to shake no. Said she cried for months over that boy. He said living was hard for her when their son was alive, and he took most of her to the grave when their child died. The shell left would not eat. Said the only thing it could do was cry itself a river to soften its journey to death awaiting arms. He told of their other child, an infant. She lived in Chicago with his sister. Said he never really got to know her. Explaining how he couldn't see much driving by his sister's house. He told how he sent his sister money for the child and hoped she'd have a good life. Said he never could force himself to stop. Not even to visit his sister. Said he did not have that right. He stated the last time he held his girl, she was in diapers. He said his life ended after watching his wife lose her will to live. He said they tried everything, but she did not want to live.

For the longest time, he just stared out at the river. He stopped talking as he kept bringing his bagged bottle to his lips. Then, out of nowhere, he said, "I had a promising life once." "I had a good life once, but my dream was a dream which was never meant to be." He said he took his girl to his sisters after his wife died and then went out to drink. He said he was drunk enough to accidentally kill a man who said the wrong thing to him. Said he was sober enough to toss him in a dumpster. Lost enough to believe everything had no meaning. He said his life simply faded away after that. After a while, he got up and told me he was an evil, confused soul. He slit Toucan Sam's throat, shot Tony the Tiger between the eyes, and made Captain Crunch walk the plank. After this, Tommy turned and walked away. I never saw him again, but I've often wondered if he was telling me he was a serial killer.

The next thing I knew, Tommy was dead. Some claimed it was from an overdose. These claimed

Tommy took his life in the woods no one talked about. A rumor began to form. It was coming to light that Tommy may have known too much. Tommy was friendly toward me, and I often think of him as a victim. I am not a victim. I am a survivor; victims have boughten into the lies others tell them.

Chapter 44

Soon after my brother's death, I was approached at school. The man said he was a teacher, but I'd never seen him around the school. He claimed to be studying to become a school psychiatrist and asked if I'd help him. He wanted me to talk with him after school on a specific day of the week. I do not remember which day it was, but it could have been Thursday. I never obtained a good feel for who he was. I wonder why someone who was training didn't have someone to watch over him during his training. I could not tell if he worked undercover, was helping Tommy's employer, or was studying to be a school psychiatrist. I did know he wanted to meet me in my old English classroom. It was one of the best rooms to get in and out of quickly if such a need arose. I agreed to talk with him. However, I did not agree to tell him anything. We would talk. He asked questions, but I refused to know anything except who would win the game Friday... Rah- Rah- Rah. Other than that, I told him everything was fine.

Tommy had walked our streets for years, and no one seemed to bother him. It was well-known what Tommy did for his existence, yet no one seemed to care. The fact that people left him alone made me wonder who Tommy worked for. The man died in those woods where no one I knew ever went. Killed in the woods where that old man said he built an A-frame cabin for the man who owned the gravel pit. Died in the woods owned by the man who I believe had one man killed and another falsely imprisoned to cover up his son's affair with the dead man's wife.

They claimed Tommy overdosed, then shot himself for good measure. I heard he didn't have any marks or powder burns. I also discovered that he wasn't wearing his trench coat and the place he stayed mysteriously burned down. People in this world will kill you for little or nothing. I never saw the need to give anyone a possible cause. No one ever mentioned Tommy's gun. The man to fill Tommy's void drove a baby blue, white rag-top suicide door Lincoln. He was a mean, nasty, big, bold, ugly guy. He owned a bar downtown where people were invited to start something he could finish. He fancied himself a finisher. Claimed to serve the coldest beer in town, but even if that were so, he'd choose to sell it to a very limited clientele. He said he was a businessman who believed in delegating segregation.

When dad was in the hospital, he couldn't talk much. He often lay in his bed with an extra blanket pulled up, convulsing and shivering. Sometimes, he would fall asleep, wake up, and look about as though he was afraid. Often, when he awoke, he looked bewildered. Dad looked confused for only a few seconds, but even on these days, if he happened to spot me, he could not bring himself to consciousness. I did not talk much. I never felt like I knew what to ask. I had no idea what would be necessary for a dying man. Besides, I hadn't figured out what I needed to know. There were times, however, when he awoke when he was not feeling like a dying man in the hospital. Sometimes, when he awoke, his mind allowed him to revisit other places or times he had been. The time I remember most is the time he awoke crying. He tried his best to convince me to get his pistol; he wanted to end his suffering. He told me how to break into his house. He told me where his 38 would be hidden. He told me to be careful because an unloaded gun was useless. He gave such details about where his gun would be. "Second drawl from the top, under the t-shirts." I listened carefully to every word; I thought he needed me to help him break out. Then he sprung his goal on me.

I had heard how men had mercifully smothered their suffering wives with pillows. I heard how they cried for mercy because they could no longer stand to see them suffer. I left in a hurry. I feared the suffering of one dying could be used persuasively against me. I feared the selfishness of such an act. It was odd because while I was leaving, I remembered all the times I had hidden, fearing the things others told me dad would do. I then discovered this fear was unlike the fear of hiding from the queens. I remember listening to my heartbeat and being amazed they could pass by so close and never hear its pounding.

Once, when dad woke up, he thought I was mom's baby brother. I did not know it then, but my American aunts and uncles mostly grew up together. Anyway, this one-time dad thought I was my uncle, begging me to skip school with him and go fishing. He started telling on himself and some of the members of mom's family. I tried to act like my uncle so he would reveal more. He said to me about shortcuts I never knew existed in one of my uncle's places. He knew of our secret fishing hole, someplace with a rope swing and a cave that went way back and was great to hide in.

After dad died, his remaining brother and sisters tried to teach me about their family. I asked if dad had ever tried to skip school. When my uncle thought about that, his face lit up, and he took to cackling like an old hen. He told of how dad and the boys tried to once. They were too young to plot it. So, the men made up a story about an old hermit who lived back in those woods. The truth was moonshiners shoot first and ask questions later. Moonshiners do not like kids running about disturbing things. He said they warned them about going too deep into the woods, looking for mushrooms. They constantly reminded them of safe boundaries. He said they overheard the boys talking one day, planning to skip school, fish, swim, and play away a day. They talked about how they would sneak over to where the girls swam. He told how they planned to sneak in and take the girls' clothes, tie them in knots, and hide them in the trees.

Then, he explained the plan the men had. He told of one of the dads agreeing to hide to help scare the boys once the secret was out. They had some guy who was able to through his voice. They had some man come to the house when all those planning to skip school were there. My uncle said the man played the part well. He told how the rumor somehow got out that the new truant officer was the governor's brother, and when he caught kids skipping school, they were in trouble. Said they laid it on thick. Told some wild story about the man's bloodhounds always took advantage of an opportunity to capture an escaped prisoner or truant child. My uncle said he told his boys and my dad that he believed them to be amongst the best dogs in the county, though he felt, at times, they were too aggressive in their biting the captured.

He told of that day the boys had planned finally coming. Of the boys, unaware of the plan some men had for them and, said of a few of the father's ability to sound like a game, and one man he swore could sound like a bobcat.

He told how the men waited for the boy to enter the woods. They began to snap branches while hiding and making strange sounds behind them. He said when the first boy turned to see what the one dad was following, they started doing his bobcat impersonation.

He told of those unarmed boys picking up sticks and how their group puckered. He was laughing so hard he had to stop telling the story a couple of times to wipe the tears from his eyes. He said those boys' eyes got as big as saucers when they started to bay like hounds. When one guy turned his dogs loose, those scoundrels took to running and were so afraid to notice they weren't bloodhounds. Said that night at supper was fantastic. His boys and my dad returned all worn out but unable to tell a soul about their day. Knowing they would be in trouble if they admitted they skipped school and went that deep into those woods. My uncle winked at me, then said, "There is no telling what some old hermit would do to boys he found snooping about his business like that."

The uncle who told me this story was a funny fellow. I was at his place shortly after one of his boys returned from the service. At the breakfast table, he looked at him and told him he'd been back long enough. Said his boy needed to start farming, or he had to go into town to get a factory job. The guy was back two or three days when this happened. Anyway, my cousin went into town. He returned about four in the afternoon. When my uncle came in and saw him, he asked if he had a job. My cousin told him he did and that he was going to be a game warden. My uncle looked at him for a while, then reached into his back pocket to pull out his billfold. He opened his billfold, handed his son a few hundred dollars, and then told him to return to town and pick out a nice black suit for his funeral. When his son enquired why. My uncle said they shoot wardens and liquor dicks back in the woods. My cousin became a rancher.

I remember when we got our first color TV. All the kids climbed in the back of dad's old pickup, and he drove us out to the zenith salesman's place. We picked a considerable counsel in the Early American styling to match our other furniture. That TV cabinet hid a radio and turn table in another part of its cabinetry. After sliding back its lid, you could see the place they had created for the record's storage. If you were to come to the house anytime during my childhood, all our furniture matched except grandma's huge recliner/rocker. That thing didn't match anything except her. She endlessly sat in it and worked on crocheting double bedspreads. First, she made the squares. After having the right amount, she would begin joining the squares together. Tirelessly, she would sit and work at those things. She sometimes did it with her eyes closed, feeling her way about her work while her foot kept the rhythm and rocked the chair. She could sit forever, making those eight-by-eight rose patterns on her squares. She could yell at us at any time and never open an eye. It didn't matter much what we did; if it involved breathing and grandma was there alone, we did it wrong. We didn't stay in much.

I remember waiting for the zenith man from the store/repair shop to deliver our new TV. We would not be straining over that little black & white thing anymore. Finally, the day came. When it came. He noticed we needed the proper antenna for our new TV. Very carefully, he explained how the Zenith manufacturer would pay for the labor if we purchased the new tower/antenna. Zenith believed we might assume the pictures' poor quality resulted from our TV, not our antenna's poor location. Before we could watch it, we had to wait for the tower to be installed. Three days for that bottom piece, and the rest took half a day. Our new building was the tallest around, and it had a motor to turn the antenna connected to a control box that sat on top of our new Zenith TV.

This setup was sweet. It was a one-man operation. I would not have to listen to my brother's yelling to relay it to the one tightening the bolt at the base of our old antenna. Finally, the day arrived when we could relax and enjoy our new setup. In those days, we had three channels. We were all gathered to watch the *Red Skelton Show*. I loved it when *the mean widdle kid* came out of his dresser drawl; my brother was like those two birds. "My instincts tell me it's time to fly south. My end sticks, but I don't keep my beak back there." A thunderstorm broke loose, and a bolt of lightning hit our antenna. Some of its electricity traveled down our wires and blew out our new TV, this caught our curtains on fire. Once again, the house had to summons the firemen.

After agreeing with the insurance man about something, the shop's salesman/repairman/owner returned to the house. He said he thought we would have a better product if we allowed him to fix it. That way, mom would not have to worry about damaging a replacement that might be sent out. Months later, he returned with our new, rebuilt, better-than-new, one-day-old burnt-out Zenith TV. Some forty years later, it was reported that the thing was still set in its place. It still claims the spot the repair man put it in on the day of its return. It only moves for cleaning and repainting purposes.

When I was a kid, I met a man who rode a motorcycle right before my brother died. A Honda 450. It was the big non-Harley bike of its day. The guy was a good man. His dad taught him his rights ended where another begins. When he moved in and didn't know anyone, he would walk out into the street and wave down people who rode bikes. After a while, the local bikers knew where he lived, and they'd drop in and work on bikes together. Sometimes, very little work got accomplished, but the talk was great. After a while, he became known as someone who could fix bikes. One day, a person came over with an old Honda 90, cream *Dream*. It had a problem in the area of its magneto. It took a little time to fix. He then asked me to get up on the thing and run it through the gears.

The guys all lined up against the walls as I climbed aboard. When I came back down through the gears, someone pushed me off the center stand and out of the garage I rode. I kept it slow and went around the building. When I started to pull in, they encouraged me to keep riding. I took that thing up the hill, out in the field. I was popping the clutch and giving it gas coming down the mountain. Some guy told me to do that going up it. That thing jumped up on its rear tire, and I had to lean way up to keep it from coming back on me. Soon, I was riding wellies. Then his neighbor came out screaming. That woman didn't like guys who rode bikes. After chewed me out for a while, she told me she would call the cops if I ever did it again.

One time, one of the cops who came over was a biker who was having trouble with his bike. He started talking to the others and forgot the time. He was telling them what was happening with his bike when a bunch of backup cops came. He apologized and told the cops what was happening. Everyone laughed a little. The cop came back another day, and they fixed his bike.

One time, that neighbor came out and climbed on me because her kids were down for their nap. I was riding a 125-dirt bike that had been bored to 175 specifications. I started to put the bike away when the biker asked what had happened. I told them all she had said. My friend told me she owned their property, not his. He went out, and they had quite an animated discussion. She stormed off after he told her that the next time she came on his property to establish rules, she better bring cash because there'd be a bill to pay. When he returned, he told me I could ride the bike again. When I went to get on the bike, one of the guys asked if we knew how the local cops checked to see if a bike was ridden. I told him they checked the exhaust pipes.

I had to postpone my ride until we had our timing down for replacing the exhaust system. The gathering dads looked like my pit crew instead of neighborhood men who rode bikes. We got it so we could replace the exhaust before the cops came. That non-muffled bike was deafening, especially while going between buildings. Time and time again, the cops would be summonsed. However, they knew us by then. They would come into the garage and talk a little but were never allowed to tell us who called, although they often nodded in her house's direction. It did seem the cops who came to check the pipes appeared to be the ones who rode. They knew who was riding, but no one else ever complained. The people around her didn't like how she tried to rule our neighborhood.

Chapter 45

I was alone at the house when two princesses and one of the victims they had captured came to aid a foolish, love-struck old woman. They strutted defiantly through the house, knowing it would never file charges against the queen and the members of her court. They knew the house's occupants; they deserved their prescribed positions. They knew they had silenced their voices, even when we tried to be heard. Still, they never suspected I had heard what they thought was said in secret. They may not have realized that people who will talk about others with you will most likely talk about you with others. They robbed her walls of pictures, paintings, and statues. They stole her shelves of family photo albums and money. They ransacked the house, looking for things to take which would cause pain. They took sentimental items. The tapes of the dead son's songs, the family bible that had carefully sat on the coffee table since the wedding day. They did this and then allowed it to be known that they neglected or destroyed what they had stolen. 'I heard how they had taken all the old broken woman had and discovered it wasn't worth the cost of having her. I heard how they used her, cashing in her burial insurance to upgrade the plumbing in their house they bought and were restoring. They took and took from the battered old woman, and after taking all she had, they returned her so she could spend her remaining years reeling in the knowledge that his love was rehearsed. I witnessed her defiantly walk into the home where my uncle once lived (on the day of his funeral) and tell his widow, "You're never too old for sex." "Love," the queens said, "Can cause a person to do crazy things." I heard how it caused them to drive that broken, betrayed woman from house to house of her children until she was received at the place she once ruled. She returned a fallen monarch. Her money was refused. She could again reside, but only because some people do what is right despite knowing it often calls upon the individual to sacrifice.

Their damage was complete; though the house appeared erect, the strings had been cut. The rape of the family members at knifepoint. The forced entry of a cousin. People were writing to the site, reaching for those self-evident truths. Desperately struggling to expose the abusers as they were forced once again to relive their past. The world was expressing its disgust. People were questioning society's unchallenged faith in a broken system that remained. The system works. Some people are well off despite the system's ineffectiveness in doing what it is portrayed to do. Their strategy worked, though it didn't do what its projected image claims. The system works through its arms do not reach past itself. Their method returns favors owed to those who support and promote the right candidate.

As the child protection agency demanded they understood what had happened in his life to permit such behavior, the FBI cast its eyes upon everyone and everything. Whenever something is said that is not their expectation, the FBI demands to know how things became so disarrayed.

Ask; our FBI is said to set the standard for investigations. I asked if they were preparing a federal case against him for human trafficking or some other infraction. Were they checking to see if all the local department's Ts were crossed and Is dotted? Were they clearing the government of any wrongdoing? Were they searching to close holes that may have been found in the system? The question they asked seemed to be concerning speculation. This sounded like, "If you were in his place, what possible explanation would you give for the behavior?" His upbringing was in question. Our world was in question. They wanted to understand what they were looking upon. The media and the websites slowed their coverage of the case. Not much was being released. Messages were recorded on Facebook by people all across the country expressing their disgust with the whole ordeal. Then another man's computer was taken to where the captured once conducted business. It was mentioned on the news earlier. Then, the information was hushed.

Another child molestation ring was uncovered in the Sunshine State. Interestingly, it was where he was rumored to have been moving. It appeared as though the authorities did not need to know his passwords to get information from his hard drives.

I was sent a link to a news real of him sitting in a courtroom. His cheeks looked as though he had been in an altercation. He sat before his judge expressionless.

I was told that when his mother visited, he didn't speak. She claims he only cries. I have heard she apologized to everyone while hanging her head. Some believe she is trying to get past the thoughts haunting her. I have been told she says she wishes he would die. I know that acts of self-preservation are prevalent. I am told he can only be visited for a half hour per week, and because of that, no one except his mother goes. Can you imagine spending your only time allotted to communicate with the outside world with someone who has repeatedly said she wishes you were dead? It seems ironic the person on trial for his life sits in a cell awaiting the moment he can escape and be with one to whom he is already condemned. Did she come to her statements because it would bring justice to the children? Was she feeling grief over what he had done? Would his death permit her to walk about, not feeling the eyes of her world were upon her? What was going through a mother's mind, past baring age, to cause her to wish for her only child's death?

The day of maneuvering by the lawyers was brought to an end. It was early morning, and the mist, along with the fog, brought the fog, but it was beginning to lift. People were starting to arrive at the courthouse before its standard opening. Months had passed with people searching the papers to find the slightest hint of when his trial would begin. These people needed to learn about the day's event. Six hours before the start of his practice, phones started to ring. The trial which would finally put the sleepy little city on the map had been scheduled to begin. The ones making the schedule did not know this day's events as they called the people who would appear during the trial. These people were too quickly and quietly gathering at the courthouse. The arrangements had been planned to help the police deal with mob control. The city was under society's microscope. I could not help but wonder if the judge realized such trickery would only work for the first day of jury selection.

At one time, our courthouse's dome was painted bright neon orange; then, it became a fluorescent green. I remembered being at the stadium, across the river, during a football game, wondering if this was the image others would want their county's justice system to project.

An unmarked SUV pulled up against the curb on the Water Street side of the courthouse. A group of men hovered over and around someone they hurriedly were trying to sneak through the back door. As this occurred, a man in an old Ford pickup with Texas plates parked his truck in the middle of the street, yelling something to the mass of bodies, "Now you will pay for what you've done to my boy. You..." Policemen formed the huddle and desperately tried to get the man in its center through one of the doorways beneath the rear stairs of the courthouse. Still, the screaming cries from the father whose son had been taken and ultimately given to the accused caused a moment's distraction. This distraction allowed for a brief separation. During that instant, the crack from a rifle echoed throughout downtown. A moment later, the accused lay silently on the cold flagstone walkway of the courthouse. The trial to answer all the questions was canceled by the impact of a single round.

The police drug his body to safety under the steps while searching the mist for the shooter they began doing CPR. People were running, trying to figure out what was happening. Some were getting out of town before the workday rush. The newspeople rushed to press against the lines of the cops. They began asking questions to get the answer they already suspected. The man in the old Ford was taken into custody. He had to be released but was commanded not to leave town. Everyone claimed no one knew how this could happen. Some in town thought he got what he deserved. His mother collapsed, asking the atmosphere what she had done to deserve the injustice. Across the river, a single person climbed unnoticed from the football stadium light tower. The cops searched the town, but the city was well-versed in not knowing such things. Some in town were saying the shooter lifted the taxpayer's burden. The man from the Ford momentarily met his ex-wife before she left. They silently spoke their pleasantries and reminisced about old, forgotten yesterdays. They kissed each other; then she turned to reenter her car. As she did so, he said, (Darling, you showed them. They best remember, don't mess with Texas".

I could allow a thousand such thoughts to unwind across my mind. I can think of several people who might want to see the man in custody dead. I know of people who believe such criminals should be given a gun with a single bullet and then advised to use it wisely. I cannot, however, imagine saying I wished anyone of my children were dead.

Another of these articles told he had once housed other children of the system. It explained how the teenage boys ran and demanded another roll of the dice, insisting they would never stay with the accused. It told that none of these boys had been questioned concerning their reason for running. This had some wondering why a forty-eight-year-old single man who had never married and was up on forty-eight counts of sex crimes against a minor under ten would want to adopt someone from a system that did not find it necessary to question others who were placed in his care, before giving him the children. Perhaps they couldn't see a possible link to those who demanded a second roll of the dice. Maybe there are other people who have things on their computers they believe are hidden.

Anyway, I agreed to talk with the head investigator from the FBI. I expressed my concerns, but I explained that I knew little of interest to her. I answered a few questions and requested that she look into a few county records. I could not help but believe there might be more to this than they were willing to allow the public to know. These people and the news on this matter were silenced. Criminal busted for sex crimes against minors were being conducted. The man they held in custody was no longer viewed as a community pillar. He would never again be allowed to coach the junior high boys' basketball team. It would most likely be complicated for him to become the president of an adoptive parents advocate agency anytime soon. The papers had claimed the case against him to be airtight. He allegedly sold his adopted son to an FBI agent.

They also reported that he suddenly suffered from a serious money problem. His leased Escalade was taken back and returned to its proper owners. His house and probable crime scene, which certain family members were permitted to enter to remove whatever they determined to be theirs. As they once did to "the house" without such permission. Then, his property was foreclosed on. It might appear to some the boy was at the front, and upon his capture, his banking arrangement quickly but silently fell through. He was some throwaway face for a service provided.

Again, my phone rang. It was someone who claimed to be the child's advocate for this case. She claimed she had received my number from the Lady in the FBI. I agreed to talk with her, but she was more interested in opinions than records to look up. I then tried to call back the Lady from the FBI to express my concerns about her giving my number out and the claims the advocate had made. I was not pleased with my number being exchanged, nor was I impressed with the advocate. I have never been called back by the FBI. I returned a call to the advocate but did so to tell her to lose my number. I realized she was all about the adopted children because she made it clear she did not care about other people. To the advocate, all others were insignificant. She wanted cold, rigid, callous, calculated opinions. I was welcomed to go back and form another view of the system in which everyone is victimized. She was all about her case studies and their meaning to her career. She made me feel like I didn't have permission to breathe.

I wished the advocate well, then told her I would not be coming to play. It is harder for me to recall the events of my past than to experience them in some respects, unlike the surreal fears that awaken me at night now when I recognize things that happened. When I force myself to remember those events, I know the outcome but cannot brace myself. I am forced to relive the events through the eyes of a child, unprotected by innocence and unable to change their courses. After all these years, after years of being suppressed, I now reach for the truth of what occurred, knowing my memory conceals another trap. I am unable to take hold of it all at once. I know all that happened wasn't bad. We had what we thought were good times. However, those things we were trained to endure and to not talk about have left scars to cloud my memories.

Chapter 46

One afternoon, one of the bikers came to tell us he had his bike stolen. I went river fishing when they pulled its frame out of the river. How the guy knew where that frame was, he never said. The serial numbers had disappeared. Somehow, he was able to get his old motor back. He found he could not register the bike because of some minor technicality concerning those missing numbers. One of the cops who visited told him he could get it registered if he told the inspectors he had built the bike. They began the re-registering process. They ground the serial numbers of the motor. Then stamped in what the bikers started calling the owner. They found out they couldn't register the engine with the frame because the inspectors would know it was the motor from a 750 Honda. This was when the rigging began. They somehow took the engine from that 90 Dream into that 750 Honda frame. Then continued to work on this contraption until it could do everything necessary to pass inspection. It only had one working gear, but it was all needed to pass the examination. We strapped it in the back of a pickup to take it over for the test. A lot of the bikers and cops followed, wanting to see this. Before taking the test, the owner put on leather gloves and a new bandanna to protect his crash skull. We had to stop short of the station so he could ride it in. The thing passed the visible part of the inspection. Then he climbed back on and slowly rode around the test course. By this time, it was the only bike any inspector was inspecting. When he came to the line, it looked like he stopped it by putting his feet down more than by its breaks. He waited a while. Then we heard the sound of its model A Ahuja horn. One of the inspectors who didn't know better asked what happened to the serial numbers. The biker told him he could never remember those things, but he knew his name. People just shook their heads and laughed, but it passed. Within a couple of days, it was back to being an excellent 750. It never got given its dubbed name, "The Lead Sled."

The rumor about the town was the owner of the bike refused to pay some gambling debt. They said he was at a bar one night and bet a cop his bike could beat the cops' racehorse in the fifty-yard dash. People who claimed to have been there said that he would have won if the race was 5 yards longer. Still, that horse broke out at full speed, and the bike had to recover from breaking traction and never reached full speed quickly enough to recover. I was there when they fished its frame from the river. The other is probably true. I saw the guy do some crazy things. Once, when cops were chasing him, I saw him ride it across the train trestle. I remember wondering why he would do it. Everyone in town knew who owned that bike, and no one else looked like him.

Chapter 47

When I became a little older, I met this kid I should have gone to school with. I am trying to remember how we met. Anyway, this kid's coloring needed to be corrected. His eyes were big, and he was as bald as a cucumber. In fact, this kid did not have any hair at all. He had to wear a mask because his treatments caused his hair to fall out. His skull had a yellowish hue but was dull and smooth looking. With his big eyes, rounded head, and tiny ears, which sunk close to the cavity his puffy skin allotted them, somehow, we became friends.

In the end, he could do much, but then it got so he could hardly do anything. The kid would drool all over himself and smack his leg when I came by. He was happy when anyone remembered to stop by. At this stage, the kid could no longer speak, but the sounds he made would change. He got all excited if you guessed what he wanted to say. It was sometimes hard to see him, mainly because I remembered how he was before the disease advanced. His body had deserted him, and his parents wondered when I would do the same. Sometimes, his eyes told me things I was unable to understand. His parents said they wanted him to die at home and not in some hospital room. That is when I learned that death is not prejudiced; it is bound to eventually come upon us all. Near the end, he didn't have the strength to slap his leg. Sometimes, he looked disappointed to still be with us when he opened his eyes. Sometimes, when they opened, he looked scared, like he'd forgotten where he was. A nurse came to make his passing as painless as possible. His room was filled with machines with flashing lights and monitors, which showed us numbers. That last day, I remember looking at people who had forgotten why we were there. It was easy to forget and get caught up in what the machines indicated. Whenever I allowed this to happen, I neglected my purpose.

I thought I had gone to help comfort him during his passing. I thought we gathered to comfort each other. Still, when I saw those readings as though they were not recording the loss of life, I felt I had betrayed myself and the others. At times, it was impossible to stand and look at the others present. It was also useless to sit. We talked to his shell, hoping somehow what we said registered. Sometimes, during that room's somber mood, someone would somehow allow a smile to break out. The person who did would relate a story concerning them and him from another day. Sometimes, people needed to step away for a moment. His parents would go over to kiss him and tell him they loved him, that it would be alright, they'd be coming shortly. I couldn't say much and could only hold his dying hand briefly. I remember thinking how odd it was that births and deaths reintroduce us to how fragile we are. I have never liked the thought of dad probably passing while in his hospital room alone. Somehow, it appears to be an insult that we allow anyone's passing to go unnoticed. It is as though we have never fully grasped the tragic beauty of life.

When my friend passed, somehow, he took pieces of his parents with him. Each mourned the loss of their son differently, yet each was no longer whole. She needed to remember. She would smile and cry at the same time. Calling for her was a good thing. When he was in the yard working, I saw him stop and stare into the air as though he had found some hidden message from his son. He would end these sessions with a nod toward the letter he'd seen. Then, he'd go about his tinkering. As a child, I knew it was not normal for parents to outlive their children. Instinctively, I knew this to be wrong. After his passing, people would visit them and accidentally say some of the cruelest things. Sometimes, words cannot reach people. Sometimes, people need to be touched. People need to know their lives hold value. Still, even now, I do not believe most people realize the hollowness or the depth of the phrase, "I do not care." I don't think we understand those words' meaning until we have suffered significant loss.

Chapter 48

After a particular queen gave birth to her only child, he came from the hospital to the house. The baby's parents stopped by on the weekend to visit. For the first years of his being, the boy was hushed by the rumbling of the house. On weekends, his parents would show up to say "Hi "and take all they could. They claimed our food and pretended to like us. The house did not seem to care about their thefts. They were considered adults; we were kids and didn't have a chance.

Once, I heard rumblings of her dressing her baby in little girl dresses after he was old enough to visit their apartment. I believe these visits allowed others to feel the house's emptiness. I was ordered to another room while some adults questioned it. We kids never heard talk of such again until they brought him back after he'd gotten into what they said were a bag of prunes. They claimed he ate himself into trouble. What I know is the child couldn't walk without needing a change. When they put him down, he started to walk and stopped to change his expression while soiling what we discovered to be little lace panties. His parents laughed at him, enjoying the humiliation. The queen stood before her throne that day to issue the decree that she had better never see the likes of that again. The child was swooped up and rushed to another room where those panties were exchanged for big boy pants. The young queen had forfeited her rights and was denied her right to pillage during her subsequent few visits. How dare anyone openly act as though the house did not uphold the appearance of normality? How dare anyone torture one of the boys of the house before they reach puberty?

I always have liked babies. I've changed their diapers, made those crazy faces, and played with babies as far back as I can remember. I cannot recall when the house did not have a baby. I understood that mom needed the baby to help her through after my brother's passing. Still, that boy is the only child I held, which did not have the promise. Most babies are magical. You can take a baby into a room full of strangers, and the baby will light the place up. Still, watching that child grow was like watching a moth play with a flame. It had nothing to do with premonitions and everything with knowing the way of the house and the world's spin.

It is true. The queen's kid was not an immaculate conception; he did have a mother and father. What a father his queen mother found. She was introduced to the subject when she went to get her mother out of the local cougar bar. She went to help the bartender encourage her mother to slither away. Or that is the way I remember her telling the story. He had been married once before to a woman older than himself. They had two children. A girl, then a boy. Something happened to their boy, and the divorce soon followed. Even after his second wedding, his first wife called him by the pet name she had for him. She claimed they would remarry once the children were out of her house.

He was arrested for exposing himself to some early teens at the local mall. The girls did not press charges. Their laughter and pointing, among other gestures, alerted the authorities. He was soon caught in the act and arrested. Grandma paid his bail with money she stole from us. I heard her tell him that he was to show her if he had something worth showing. Soon after, they openly displayed their affair before all. His wife was in her mid-twenties, he was in his early forties, and our grandma was in her late eighties. There were rumors that he molested his nieces and nephews.

However, through it all, I recall the torture of trying to fit in. Somehow, I knew I would never make it. We may have appeared close, but never when I did not feel the distance. Even when the monsters pretended to accept me, I never felt acceptable. No matter how hard I tried, there was a distance. In my child's mind, a family was supposed to function as a body. Our bodies would have been monstrous.

Adults devour their children and any other child in their wake. Still, there is something strange about such interdestruction. I always wondered why it is so drawn to itself. The queens had a way of finding men who longed to be humiliated and controlled. These men needed to appear proper in public, though they had to be far from their appearance privately. The main trouble with this philosophy was their version of normal seemed different. When one part of their body hurts, the others must cover for it. Distort the truth and promote the lies. That created the strangest view of the ordinary in history. Although standard in a leper colony is leprous. As children, we were unable to grasp what was happening. Teachers were trying to teach us. We were trying to find our way, and the constant conflicts brought our silence. We were told elaborate, frightening tales concerning my dad, our grandfather, and his dad. The only thing I knew concerning my grandfathers I found by searching the web.

Dad raised me to fight back. I am not saying he introduced us to fight back, but he raised me that way. He probably did so because he wished he had. Dad must not have known fighting isn't always the answer. He told me briefly about life as he knew it to be while I was passing through his hospital rooms. It took me years to figure out some of the things dad said. When he'd go to the used car lot as a small child, dad often would take me. He taught me to question everything. He taught me to challenge the presented reality. "Reality is not what is expected," he'd say, "It may be the concept of reality, but it does not make it real." You can run from reality, hide from reality, deny reality, remain blind to reality, and yet the reality is. Despite it all, the reality is. Reality will not change for an individual. The question I perceived the authorities wanted an answer to was, "How did they allow such crimes to occur?" In reality, society not only permits them but also nurtures them.

I was told about his being taken into custody over the phone. I read it for myself on the website, and people everywhere were in a state of controlled outrage. How could they allow a forty-eight-year-old single man to adopt three children in a relatively short period? Also, why was he permitted to move them thousands of miles from everything they knew? These children were taken from their state's confirmed abusive families and forced thousands of miles from all they had ever known. It was assumed by the authorities the children wished to be a part of what the state thought to be a typical family. If the children were taken while screaming and fighting, it would be assumed their adverse behavior would be considered the acts of those who do not know what they truly need. I cannot recall once in all the years of their questioning being asked or told what a typical family was. Their state asked the new state to verify they would receive an everyday life. Then, upon signing a few forms and after a few inspections, the man was given custody of the children of families who did not know him. He returned to the former state requesting funding to send his formally abused children to his private school. He was awarded it.

They discover the abuse of these children from an advertisement he ran on Craigslist. How long do you imagine he had been conducting business to be willing to list such services on the World Wide Web? How prevalent do you suppose his crimes were amongst his circle of influence? No doubt his behavior was acceptable to others about him, or he would not have been comfortable with his actions. Who was his clientele? Why were the children who had stayed with him briefly but refused to remain under his care never questioned? How could the two men possibly be arrested for abusing their child on different dates? Yet we are told he is cooperating and that it only occurred once?

Could the appearance of their captured criminal possibly be more important than protecting the unalienable rights of children? Do those captured men complete his list, or are they merely the throwbacks from his circle of influence? When and how is it that he becomes an abuser? Why did the website close to the letters pouring in concerning his case? How is it that a state that failed these children's unalienable rights given them by their creator has the right to the children it denied the rights to? The state could not provide them with an environment to obtain life, liberty, and the pursuit of happiness. How was this able to happen?

We, our society, permitted it. If we do not collectively raise our voices, it will happen again.

Chapter 49

I recall there was a road in my hometown that was lined by giant old shade trees. I remember it because the trees never allowed their blacktop to reach the whole summer's temperature, which other roads did. This little road wound its way over a picture-perfect country bridge that leaped a small stream. It was complete with small rolling hills through green meadows and was there so people could enjoy a slow, comfortable ride. However, this road cut through a small, wooded area, which hid a danger lurking within its grassy fields. It would have been dreamlike for coasting a bike through, except for one fact. It held a blind curve that ended at the intersection of another road. The road it intercepted did not have a stop sign, but people needed to know the road to know its hidden danger. This road, which rolled through a lazy countryside was a shorter, more pleasant route to a weather community. The mayor lived there and never saw the need to erect a stop sign which would interfere with the pleasantness of going home. Children on bikes and cars periodically were in accidences. Still, all pleas from the town were denied, overturned by the small but affluent community.

The local paper reported it happened at 3:45 pm. A child on his way from school was struck by a car that tried to avoid the child. The driver did not have time to come to a stop. It said the brief clearing rain had caused a film to coat the road with a thin layer of fluids dropped by the cars, and there was nothing anyone could have done to prevent the tragedy.

People knew speed was not an issue.

In a moment, our mayor went from being the proud father of a third grader to being the surviving member of a third grader killed by a car he'd purchased. Before the sod had sent down roots, the mayor's wife was dangling from a limb of one of the trees, highlighted by the flashing lights of the road's new three-way stop. They claim a note was found in the grasp of her English teaching hand. They said it held a simple message, though it needed proper grammar. If the letter said what I heard. Her words may have formed a partial sentence. Language experts claim her words to be ambiguous. They would have believed its message to have needed to be clarified, for they would not have known if the implied message called for one of the words to have been a pronoun or a verb. City Hall chose not to through its plea out as it had the others. Even though it was not filled out on the proper form. However, there was no denying its message. It was easily understandable to any who desired to hear it. It read, "Too late."

When I entered the second grade, there were two second-grade classrooms. I went to the room on the left. It had an old, knotted, crocked, disfigured teacher who taught her students to read by sight. In the other room, a young lady taught her students to sound out words. Their teacher brought them treats, and she had ways that they claimed to make learning fun. My teacher smacked me across the knuckles whenever she caught me using my left hand to write. Second grade is where we were divided. The kids who could read by sounding out were told they were advanced. We were informed we would become a fine machinist in the factory and other meaningless parts of the system. It did not matter how well we did; we were destined to become what they had determined we would be. My sister always attended a math or science problem in high school. She obtained the highest score in her graduating class. Still, they determined she could not be their valedictorian because she was a girl and one of us. They chose the doctor's boy as their valedictorian, though he had the third-highest score. During second grade, I heard my relatives and the school authorities question what type of life I could have, seeing how I was the fourth child of a divorced woman. I could hear the adults outside our family and family members mumble about how lucky we were to have grandma living with us. These people were not ignorant; they chose to remain blind.

Chapter 50

One evening, it must have been about my fourth-grade year, we heard an explosion. It happened during the day when the night was beginning to settle. It was during the time of a specific war called a police action. I believed we had air superiority. Still, I questioned whether or not they had flown over and dropped a bomb. Then again, I had never heard of a plane, so I went to investigate. When I got outside, I could see the reflection of the fire truck lights on the houses in our neighborhood. The explosion occurred on the part of our street hidden from my view.

When I approached the scene, the firemen had two teenagers which I knew stretched out on the lawn. The third teenage member of this family was sitting on their neighbor's steps. At the same time, another fireman shined his light into her eyes. The two boys stretched out, had little cuts all over their faces, and behaved oddly. Still, all things being considered, they lived through the blast, so they were doing all right. All the kids from that house were older than me. Their dad had died years before in some construction accident. They were being raised the best their mom knew how, which I thought would explain their getting into mischief. When I was a kid, the masses viewed any child not being raised by both a mother and father as unable to obtain an everyday life. They were alone because the mother had met some nice man who didn't mind the fact she had three teenage children. People said they fell in love, anyway, they married. After the wedding, they all got new clothes, and on Friday nights, they went out to eat at places where you only paid for the meal after it was eaten. People said he was a good man. Then the kids got new bikes and other things along with the clothes.

It was one of the other things that helped create the explosion. The stepdad had bought the boys a pellet gun. One that could be pumped up so it could shoot through the sears catalog. He and his wife decided to go out to eat. The boys decided to stay home and practice shooting. Somehow, they still need to catch up on the catalog. The pellet ricocheted and hit a pipe down in the basement where their target range was. The pellet's ricochet hit the basement light. One of the boys decided to light a match to see if to replace the shot-out bulb, but the leaking gas from the pipe the ricochet hit first ignited and blew their house off its foundation. The front door was also blown out, along with several windows. The bookworm they had for a sister was so disturbed that she had to stop reading her book. It all was happenstance. Luckily, no one was seriously hurt, not even the house, though it no longer sat squarely on top of its foundation.

I liked those guys. Shortly before the explosion, they had built a three-story treehouse in their backyard. They didn't put steps up to their treehouse. They said it was because they didn't want little kids climbing up and getting hurt. On the second floor of the treehouse, there was a little patio with a rope swing tied way up in the tree. You could swing out over their backyard, or you could swing and land upon the back-porch roof. Whenever adults caught us doing it, they would stop and tell us not to do it again. When I was a kid, it seemed that every adult in the neighborhood confused themselves with being your parent. Mostly, we ignored their request because we thought we knew what we were doing. Then, one of the older guys from the block panicked while on the rope. He mistimed his dismount. He missed the roof completely, but his foot found its gutter. The gutters spike held his foot in place, though his body was twisted as he hung upside down, screaming at the top of his lungs. The next-door neighbor and some other men from the neighborhood came to rescue him. After they did their good deed, they ratted us out. The mom of those guys who built the tree house and blew up their house took to crying and waving her hands about the air. Her new husband helped her get through everything. Still, he took down the rope the next day then helped destroy the treehouse.

A man who was dirt poor when he was growing up, though now he was one of the wealthiest in town, bought their blown-up house. He and his two sons would fix it like many others. Sometimes, they set to sell them, but a lot of the time, they kept them to rent out. I watched them at work. They went into the basement, and after nailing blocks into place between the floor joists, they used floor jack and pipes to lift the entire house. After it was up, they positioned bottle jacks and jacked them over. They took their time at work but fixed that basement and lowered the house onto it. They gave the place a brand-new kitchen. They built a little room outside the back porch's door to house the hot water heater. They tore out that old wooden front porch and made a brand-new concrete one. People said one son was normal but claimed the other to be mildly retarded. He did talk a little slower than the others, but he was good at concrete and block work and checkers. Mom worked with their sister, and she claimed they were friendly people. The so-called normal son had once been in a bad accident where someone died, so he didn't talk much until after we all got to know each other by our first names. They worked at rebuilding the house all summer long. They pulled sandwiches from a giant lunchbox and packed sodas in an excellent metal red cooler. The dad paid each of his children the same. Everyone in their family had jobs and got an equal share of the money. Whether it was rented out or sold, they each were paid the same. Their dad said he believed in each doing their part. By doing so, they ensured their family's success. They approached their obstacles as a team. They were not allowed to manipulate themselves into positions where they appeared to be over the others in their family.

Once, a group of kids from our neighborhood wanted to take a little trip, so we waited in a nearby wooded area. The woods were by the trains that came into our part of town after blowing their whistles and slowing themselves to an adjusted city's speed before crossing city streets. After that first one, we began to ride the freight trains all summer. We learned not to ride flatbeds, though they were easier to hop. These cars did not offer privacy and were the easiest to be caught on to. Therefore, we hopped aboard boxcars.

To catch the trains, we only needed to rush them as they went by. We learned to watch the other cars to ensure we would not be hit by something hanging over, such as a strap. We also learned to boil the strap pieces before making train whistles. We took samples of the straps into the house, and at night, we would boil them to sterilize the strap and get rid of their oily film. We broke these pieces into sections, which, when bent into, would bend at a hole and give an additional hole at the top and bottom. We practiced putting our tongues between these holes and lightly biting down to learn to play these whistles. The whistles were loud, shrill, desired, and free for us, or so we thought. Our authentic ones came from those who were skilled at hopping trains. Those cheap substitutes were from the straps their fathers brought home from the factory after unloading the train's cargo. Though we could never explain why we could distinguish our whistles from the cheap imitations, we were able to sell ours to our classmates. A few fathers tried to help their kids break. Still, they only partially succeeded because we manipulated the market to keep the demand up for our authentic whistles. A lot of times, we hoped those trains looking for our whistle materials. Still, we had much of the needed material and used any excuse to hop on a train. There was something about jumping on one of those powerful trains, though we were going nowhere. The freedom we felt while riding atop a boxcar rolling through the world, anticipating the release of a ride.

We would lay on the walkway while moving through the cities, but when the country air hit us, it brought a game of tag. Because of the train's ability to pick up speed, we'd get to moving along at a pretty good clip. This made leaping from car to car easier.

We had our train-hopping skills. All we needed to do was time our run to get beside one. Then we'd reach out and grab onto one of the ladders at the ends of the boxcars. The speed of the train would pull us. Then, we used the hand-over-hand technique to climb the ladder until our feet could catch one of the rungs. When we felt ourselves being pulled by the trains, we kicked out our feet during the pull to ensure their safety from the train's wheels.

Those ladders took us atop the trains where the expanded steel walkways were. When you were there, you needed to stay alert because of limbs, bridges, wires, tunnels, and the like. I took those trains for miles in each direction and never got to ride through a tunnel, though I tried. It was nice to lay flat and relax, waiting for the obstacles to pass. The feel and sounds of riding through one of the bridges with its top members were excellent. We were on such a journey one day when a guy who did not wish to be tagged mistimed his jump. He claimed, but in reality, he left the safety of the walkway and leaped from the unsure footing of the steel roof. His lack of understanding of the rules concerning jumping from walkway to walkway cost him. It introduced him to the ladder handrail system in the center of the ends of the boxcar in a rather intimate manner. When he landed his jump, a rung on the ladder had a sharp edge that sliced open his leg. He grunted while falling between the cars before his hands caught the ladder. The game of tag ended, and we helped him atop the train, where we all gathered to plan our return trip and to doctor his leg. We all agreed not to talk about it to anyone. When we returned, we each searched for the needed supplies to clean his wound and give it butterflies to keep that section of skin from flapping. The next day, he showed us his leg. The thing was getting huge, and its color changed into this strange, shiny, pale mass of colors. Puss kept the thing from healing correctly, and the dark colors along the edge of the flap were feeling harder than skin usually does.

Someone from inside our group ratted us out to their parents. I've always believed it to be one of those treehouse boys with the new dad. With the bum leg, the boy's father stormed our fort and demanded that his son come out immediately. After looking at the portion, he stopped yelling out of sympathy. Then, they rode off in their family car. The next time we saw him, the fears we had when we heard his dad's voice were confirmed; we had to go and face his dad. The stupid rat gave information about the guy's leg and told who was in the game.

Whoever that double-crosser was told on himself so he'd be called in with the rest of us. After we'd arrived, there were seats for each of us. We were not the ones talking. When the father did appear, he'd informed us there would be no more train rides. He thanked us because he claimed the doctor said we probably helped his son keep his leg through our fumbling. If not his life. He then asked us to rat out anyone who was hurt and promised he would not turn us into our parents. He promised to help us take care of our injuries, even if it meant he paid our doctors' bills. The man was good for his word. Mom probably doesn't know I was stabbed in the gut by an ice pick. I knew not to tell. It would have done no good to say anything concerning that relative. It would have made it more challenging to survive the others. Still, that dad turned out to be a good man; he solved many of our problems and was known to claim he was a kid once.

A young couple with a baby moved near us. I liked them. He worked in the factory where mom worked, although it was a different shift. His dad was our local long-hair-hating barber. If your hair was past your shoulders, he'd give you a free military buzz if he caught you. It was a game to allow him to catch a glimpse of us before disappearing. His son, our newest neighbor, was a nice guy. Mom called him and his wife, "kids just starting out." One night, they had a party, and one of the guys got so blasted he wouldn't go in, so they let him sleep in the front yard. Some other guys ran into their houses to take their wives or girlfriends' makeup supplies. They came out and painted him, so to speak. Man, he was an ugly girl. Perhaps it was because they didn't know the colors of his skin type. It looked much harder to paint fingernails and toenails than I thought. He was not very happy about their makeover when he awoke. His wife said they had to hurry to her mother to pick up their kid, so he had to go like that.

I habitually went to their house to see the man leave for work. Then, I'd play with the baby as the wife cleaned the house. Once, when I thought I wanted to take up smoking, she allowed me to hide my cigarettes there. I didn't get to the place where I enjoyed smoking. I quit as soon as I had finished the first few packs. I did not want outside pressure to allow me to pick it up again, so I told mom after securing her word. She asked all the time if I had smoked that day.

One Halloween, my friend next door and I decided to go out trick or treating. When we spotted the wife walking their little girl, we decided to hide and scare her daughter. She was due to deliver their second child at the time. My friend hid in some bushes, and I hid behind the egg-nourished maple tree. I waited to hear her footsteps and her little girl talking to her. I jumped out to scare them. The woman had a substantial hidden watermelon knife she waved over my head twice. Then she doubled over and grabbed her stomach. When she looked up, I knew to get mom. When mom came out, she told me to get the baby in the house and watch her. The lady was screaming, so mom took her to the hospital. Mom knew not to wait for help. Even through her tears, as she got into the car, she looked over and told me she was alright. When her husband came to get their little girl the following day, he told me his wife and new baby were fine and they'd be home in a few more days. I played with their daughter until they moved away into a lovely house in the country by his parents. They moved away before their second child could crawl.

There was a cop in my hometown who would look for me. He would pull over and give me a ride to the house if it was late or getting late. He never asked questions. He just looked out for me. After he called it in, I was allowed to ride in the front seat. One of the cops in our town was a friend of bikers. He was our high sheriff. Some guy broke out of the hospital's mental ward and shot him. The entire town was torn up over it. That cop was a great man. After the shooting, there was a big hunt for the shooter. People said if the shooter saw the bikers coming in his direction, he better run to a cop.

When this happened, a girl lived by my elementary school in one of the cities that swallowed up farmhouses. We had gone to her place to see if we could convince her to sneak out. Her dad saw us. We were trying to escape when we discovered their backyard close-line. That thing took my feet from under me. I limped and low-crawled into their barn while searching for cover. Though the others and I low crawled into their barn, we left at a full sprint. We found a cop, and they went to the barn and got the shooter. We were never asked how we knew he was in their barn.

I had a teacher in the ninth grade who was a lousy English teacher but a terrific guide. It really wasn't an English class. I was the only ninth grader in the class.

The others were primarily juniors and seniors. She wanted us to read books, articles, poems, newspapers, lyrics of songs, and other things. She was more concerned about our knowing the proper method of writing than obtaining the ability to express what we wanted to convey and understand what others were saying. She was amazed I liked the Raven. I did additional research about the man who wrote it for his father, even though he was another who used his pen to map his course through history. I liked Thomas, but he was better understood at night when the day ended and I was spent. That lady wore long, flowing, colorful, airy dresses and skirts. She was a lousy teacher but a trustworthy guide. She did not pretend to hold the answers. She listened and heard what words could not say. Once, when I gave an answer, she claimed I was wrong, yet to this day, I believe she knew she was and was trying to get me to defend my stand. That lady understood how to contact us to open up to expose our thought processes. I was unwilling to expose mine that day, so I told her to kiss my rosy red... She roared with laughter. The lady was true to herself. She taught by living in full view. I could call her and talk with her. She was a lousy English teacher, but her eyes were opened. I believe she cared. Her class was called English, but it was about life.

That lady had us memorize words we rarely used. She showed us how to arrive at the root of a word. She told us the origins of words are pictures and to continue searching until we discover their view. The lady understood my abuse of English. Loved its lack of diction. If I were to honor a teacher, it would go to her; though she was a lousy teacher, she was a trustworthy guide. Some in the school said she was senile. She was indeed different. Her hair was short. In some modernized pixie-type thing, but it was not a bob. She wore large dangling earrings, which many of the students in the school admired. It appeared she preferred hammered silver over the polished jewelry most women wore. She wore primarily outfits that called for belts, and her straps had massive buckles. Her clothes seemed to flow with her. She wore light sandals instead of dress shoes. She wore bright colors, reds, purple greens and blues, and occasionally the darker shades of brown. Her skin was snow white. It almost looked like she had bleached it, but it appeared soft. She did not have crow's feet, though she displayed laugh lines. She didn't bother putting on fake eyelashes, but she had her own style for applying makeup. She used bright colors that went with her attire in contrast to her skin tone, but it worked. The lady was as colorful as her look.

She would glide into the room after holding the door open, waiting for us to enter.

She never took a role, though she always knew who was missing. If she spoke to you, she was speaking to you. It was concerning you and not the student entering her room. Sometimes, she'd talk to students in class, but usually, she'd talk with us as individuals. We thought it was odd that she stopped eating meat because her husband was one of the town's best butchers. Her lunch came in a brown paper bag, but it had to be assembled at the table. She preferred to eat with us rather than with the teachers. She ate salads with wheat germs and sprouts. The other teachers and staff did not truly appreciate her, but she had the degrees. As far as degrees go, she had the best in our school's systems English department, but they would have to acknowledge her or make her the head of the department. The person closest to her regarding degrees was the speech/ theater/debate teacher. He looked like a slightly aged student. By outsiders, he might have been confused with a hippie. Though he loved his jeans and solitude, he liked being in charge. He did have long hair, a fully groomed beard, and never wore teacher's ties. The man never got excited. He was a local prodigy who received a full ride from a West Coast College. He left our town a scholar and returned a human. She was older than he was, but they seemed to like each other.

They were natural searchers who were unafraid to admit they had no answers. Neither he nor she saw the need to play the games; they simply were who they were and who they were as people who tried to expand the thinking of others. They understood abstract. The things they said or the things they had us read were mind-blowing. They did not care if I agreed or disagreed; they simply wanted to know if I understood the thought process. They could allow another being to arrive at their own conclusions. After a year with her, he recruited me for some undefined class to which only eight students were invited. He had us explore all types of literature. I knew then neither of these two stood a chance of being recognized for who they were. Still, they endured the system for the hope that sometimes seemed to glimmer in someone's eyes. Between the two of them, she would be my favorite. She was definitely the most colorful and came to class ready to explore. Her eyes were always open. She came with anticipation like a child about to experience her first carnival.

She assigned us words to master. She handed out our test with the following instructions once. Use each of the talks given Monday in a proper sentence. She did not tell us the words. We were to know them, and her providing them would have given us the appropriate spelling. I did remember the words even though it was mid-week. Try as I did, I could not recall what one of them meant. I thought I knew the spelling, so I wrote, "Mrs._____, Have I spelled _____ correctly?" She marked it wrong. I protested because I followed her instructions. She got upset and escorted me to my guidance counselor's office.

When he agreed with me, she had to change her grading of my paper. Most teachers would have laid low to get me on something else, but not her. She laughed on our way back to class and apologized for her actions. In the first grade, we sometimes drew pictures of things instead of the usual show-n-tell. I drew an overhead view of a cloverleaf interstate ramp system. I tried to explain what it was as my dad had shown me, but my classmates laughed and refused to understand. That teacher screamed to the others that she was in control. She demanded their laughter stop. They laughed at her and forgot about my picture. All I know is if you have to yell, you're in control; you are not. My ninth-grade English teacher did not say a thing, but she was in control.

Chapter 51

An old man who lived on the corner, across from the school's playground. They lived in a New England-style brick home. When I met him, he was retired and busied himself keeping up their house and property. He wore an ordinary worker's uniform. The dark gray ones were his preference, though occasionally, he wore a navy blue one. He would walk the hills during the spring, looking for mushrooms. Kids were afraid of him. He was primarily a quiet man who would longingly watch us play. He never did anything wrong, though he was a tall man who walked rigidly upright. He did not move like an old man, yet he acted as though he thought of himself as one.

He had a little cart he pushed about their lawn to transport the weeds to the trash or spread manure over their property. I was walking by one day, and though I didn't know why I spoke, I said, "Hi." I most likely was clowning around, but it startled the old man. His wife scurried into their home only to return with some freshly squeezed lemonade. The type of lemon aide with the pulp so you could find little things to chew. She only spoke briefly to ask if I wanted something she had prepared for us. One had to listen to them real close because their accent was heavy. They were friendly people, mostly quiet, and kept to themselves. However, they would have preferred to have been more social.

Later, I discovered they had never been accepted. They did some strange things, or they strangely did some things. It was easier to talk about them than to try to understand their ways. I thought it to be wrong. Someone up that invisible chain might have condemned them. They may have done something wrong but may have helped a fallen soldier. They did something to want to leave all they knew and never talk about it to come to a land they did not know. The man was proud he made his papers. This meant he became a citizen. They never asked why I spoke that day, and I do not know.

After I did, he looked for me.

Sometimes, he'd call me over to teach me something. He taught me to try to get the whole root of the weed, "for it does no good to get those tops." He taught me the way to prune roses. He explained why it was better to water in the morning than evenings. Everything the man did, he did well or paid someone to do it. I once asked him why he didn't do some other things. He said he did not do them well. I told him to practice, and he'd improve. He said, "Why bother?"

His speech was sharp and often sounded brutal. Even when he was trying to help, he said rough. It was almost like he was unsure of the strength of his words, but he could not hold back his need to communicate.

He barked out his sentences. This is what I believe scared kids. They listened to his words but ignored the man and his struggle. When he tried to speak, he tried hard at first not to say the wrong thing, which seemed all he could say. The funny thing was he had these false teeth, which must have been too big for his gums. I used to watch his mouth when he spoke because sometimes his teeth closed before his gums. Sometimes, when he pronounced a P, his teeth almost came out, but he quickly smacked them back in. I was the only person I knew of that they ever received. It was odd how they had left their country to be rejected by ours.

The respectable Stranger who pinned, "We hold these truths to be self-evident, that all men are created equal, that they are endowed by their creator with certain unalienable rights that among these are Life, Liberty and the pursuit of happiness, is said to have possessed more than four hundred humans, in his lifetime. The man who first pinned the words was as much a walking contradiction as we. It may be factual that upon his arrival at the house of Burgess, he attempted to side with an older member to abolish slavery. It may be factual the members of that house ruined the old man while viewing his infraction as belonging to someone who did not understand. It may be accurate that the British introduced slavery to America for her own gain.

Do facts alter the truth?

It would be easier to stand back and scorn Jefferson, but we do not know why he didn't free his slaves. He may have viewed his slaves as being better off with him. Blacks could not be released in Virginia at the time they lived. The common man was free in Britain, but such freedom was in a technical sense only. It does not matter how much we study; nothing alters the fact he knew slavery to be wrong. He wrote it could only destroy a nation if corrected. Some say it almost did and call its attempt the Civil War.

When Jefferson was asked to write directions for establishing the Northwest Territory, his suggestions were only overruled at one point. He would have abolished slavery by 1780. If that had occurred, it would have changed our history. We may have avoided the Civil War. Slavery was introduced to America because of greed and a lack of respect for life. It does not matter that every empire before us had slaves. America allowed slavery to exist and brought its horrors to a new level. The blood that stains our soil will scar the land forever.

The man who pinned all men are created equal allowed himself to become enslaved by the opinions of his day. He understood when he chose his words yet refused to embrace their truth. Some folk argues that the cost would have been too great. What is the value of one of the lives which was lost? The discovery of truth is a call to action. I have yet to hear anyone dare claim Jefferson did not perceive it as such. The act of one man who understood and did not embrace the truth allowed evil to continue to affect a nation. All things left to themselves deteriorate.

Chapter 52

While I was a teen, my family must have viewed me as a monster. I overheard talk concerning myself. When a new person was introduced to the family, it was me the family was concerned with. Their topics were focused on what I would say. How would I react, or how would they accept? I was not one to stir up trouble, but I would not run from it either. If I felt the cause worthy, I would calculate the degree of punishment my actions were liable to create before I dropped a bomb. Then, with certain family members, it became a game to me. Mattering little, whether the view was perceived to be right or wrong, what mattered was that they knew I was willing to stand. It was informative to study their actions, read their frustrations, and predict their next move. In time, their efforts were predictable. Still, for the most part, after study, most are predictable. We like to say we are independent, but we are interdependent. One's own studies may show where the hidden connections lie.

The art of abstract thinking demands that one removes oneself from an equation. Studying people's actions and allowing oneself to remain in the equation contaminates the study. It baffled me how anyone chose to exist, to allow themselves to become reduced to functions to obtain the moment's desires in exchange for their life. Some view their existence as all there is. I chose to explore what might become. It mattered little to me that they viewed me as being monstrous. In some ways, it was preferred. It was the reflection of my rejection of their views.

I taught myself by observing others how to fish. After the bait was cast, I could reflect upon or plan my next move. I was unsure whether I was a realist who could dream or a dreamer who could not escape reality. If the moment contained all of life we could hold, then life's illusion went far beyond absurd. I liked to explore the abstract, but I could not permit myself the luxury of fantasy.

I remember being asked, "If a tree fell in the forest and no one was around, would it make a sound?"

I pondered if sound only existed in our ears. Sound is the result of vibrations. Could a tree in the forest fall and not produce a vibration? I would have much rather known if the effects of these vibrations ever diminish. Because we know for every action, there is an equal and opposite reaction. If this is true, then the result of the tree falling is still detectable somewhere. Ripples on water met death at their shoreline, but vibrations in space may continue forever. Put another way, when would the vibrations from the fallen tree meet its shore? I would rather discuss the possibility of sound waves escaping, being captured by our ears, and never dying. Is every sound ever created still traveling through space?

The cases against the accused were closed. They were completed in both counties. They were not dropped. They were not tried. They were closed; however, the man remained behind bars. They were closed without a hint of an explanation as to what closed meant.

Chapter 53

Grandma had two living sisters. One in Kentucky and the other in southern Ohio. Both of her sisters married men with the same first names. Those two men, personality-wise, could not have been further apart. My Kentucky great-uncle loved people, and kids were included. He gave us money to walk to the country market to get ourselves treats. He talked with us. He taught us life lessons through the spinning of yarns. The man could tell a tall tale.

He told my brother and me that babies came from the cabbage patch. He claimed he had a special knife his daddy gave him long ago and then showed an old pocketknife. It was his grandfathers before his daddy owned it, he claimed. He kept the knife in a special little pocket. Its blade was not shiny. Its edge was curved by use. Though it looked dull, he warned us it was razor sharp. I knew this to be true because it was the same knife I saw him whittling with. He told us he took that knife out of his pocket while walking through the garden with my great-aunt when he was younger. It was there they saw their firstborn. He was no bigger than the tip of your little finger. He was peeking out from under a great big old cabbage leaf. He told us how my great aunt held and pulled back the leaves so he could see that little rascal better. It was then he decided to take out his knife, and with the skill of a surgeon, he cut free their firstborn. Carefully, she took their baby and warped him in a small piece of cloth she had torn from her skirt. He told us he was nervous as she swaddled him. Said that the baby was tiny, and he knew life was much too delicate to be held in our hands. He said though he was a little baby, he grew up to be a strapping man. Then he said he remembered being all thumbs while my great aunt prepared that special place mothers have for babies right behind their hearts. The man could spin a yarn. I cannot tell them as he could.

My brother and I headed to the country store later than this account. Somehow, my brother started talking to some kid.

That boy tried to tell us his version of where babies came from. I tried to correct the fool, but he insisted on his crazy beliefs. My brother and I were doing pretty good at proving him wrong when, out of the blue, he told us our great-uncle was a liar. We beat the dog out of that kid and his friend.

The next time my uncle gave me change for the country store, it came with directions. He did not want us to go fighting anyone who disagreed with us. My uncle never told on us, but ever since that fight, he took it upon himself to teach us other things. Things like the proper way to behave and how my aunt would shrink him the screw him into the light socket to send him to the moon in a light bulb rocket ship, so he could trade the man on the moon for cheese. Told us the man on the moon would not eat another bite of that bitter moon cheese once he tasted my great aunt's smooth Kentucky hand-churned butter.

My great-uncle was a funny guy. He could get the adults to laugh almost at will. He'd do so by beginning to tell his story and occasionally asking kids, "Do you know what happened next." We were right so much that he had me believing we had ESP. He was a great man. Lived his own life and helped whenever he saw someone needing help. He also schooled us when needed.

My other great-uncle with the same name was a quiet and awkward man. They had horses across the road in another field. I used to ride the black one. They also had an open-air storage area outside of their back door. Its walls were filled with exciting tools, but we could never touch them. Whenever we asked what something was, he always said, "I don't know." That back wall was filled with tools; he expected us to believe he did not know what they were. Mom said they used to be his grandfather's and were willed to him along with a blacksmith shop.

On one visit, I went outside and was peddling the sharping stone. When that great uncle saw me, he asked if I could turn it faster. When I did, he jogged over and got something from the wall to sharpen; then he came back to put edges on the things he didn't know what they were. When I questioned him, he said, "Waste not want not."

I didn't like having to go there. It never felt comfortable. These relatives tried to be outwardly polite, but I could feel we were not welcome. My great-aunt never had a good word for my grandpa. The man was dead years before I was born, but this fact never slowed her down. She would harp on the man as though her complaint against him were committed yesterday. I don't think she was particularly fond of his wife. She'd tell us that our grandma was a spoiled baby sister when she knew she could get away with it. She complained about her and her husband having to pay five dollars more than any other child in their family to bury their mother and did not think it fair the lot fell upon them because she was the eldest. Five dollars must have been a lot of money for her to treat her sister as she did for over forty years.

Grandma would sit silently in a kitchen chair and coward down to her attacks. She would complain about our grandpa and tell how her husband's parents worked for Governor Taft before he was President. For some reason, she did not care to explain they were given their choice of household belongings when he was called upon to move to Washington. They chose a picture of the Indian Princes, which hung behind their piano, which never was played.

Their house had those big wooden beads of various sizes, shapes, and colors hanging in the doorway between the living room and the hall, which led to the bedrooms. And bath. The college called her when they needed help solving a math problem. They claimed she was brilliant. I did not see it. Treating us as she did. Her youngest girl lived next to her, but their yards were divided by a small gulley that did not have a stream in it, though it had a small footbridge to pass over. Their son had a little house up the road a piece. The doctors at the state college studied him. He was also considered intelligent but a lot older than me.

Every time we went, it seemed grandma couldn't recall how to get to their house. I don't think she ever really wanted to go. We started heading in that general direction and went until we found something that looked right. Once this was accomplished, it seemed okay to drive on in. Grandma couldn't sit still as we grew closer. It was almost as though you could hear the screaming of the photos of dead presidents, which grandma kept in her purse as we turned into their drive. They were the stingiest people I've ever met. I never wanted to go there. I always left their place starving because I couldn't eat with them, not t I sure was not eating anything she cooked, not that I recall her ever offering a morsel.

One of the last times I went there, their son and I went mushroom hunting in one of their fields down by a river's edge. The land was near a natural marsh and had some trees downed by a storm the year before. It should have been an excellent hunting place, but I couldn't. He took multiple bags to keep the mushrooms separated as they were picked. He also turned his car off whenever we came to a downhill grade. As we walked across the field into where we would look, I enquired why he turned the car off those times. I was slightly concerned after seeing him struggle through the turns. He said his momma wouldn't pay for the gas to go downhill. I asked why he carried so many bags to go mushroom hunting. He said he didn't always know which ones were poisonous, so they kept their mushrooms separate and fed a few from each bag to a caged chicken. If the chicken died, they didn't eat those mushrooms. I walked back to their house and never went hunting with him again.

It was not a welcoming house. I could feel the steam of hatred boiling off my great aunt's caldrons. Whenever she caught me away from the protection of witnesses, she approached as a cat would approach its prey. She must have felt it to be some sacred duty to deliver messages about my grandfather, which she claimed I needed to know. When she spoke to me, it was never good, and mostly about subjects I was defenseless. I couldn't change the outcome of what she warned me about, even if I agreed. She told me she spoke out of love and thought I needed to know my heritage. If my family speaks to you out of love, duck. She claimed my grandparents were no good. Then told how grandpa was voted the best-dressed man in the county but was no good. Said he showed such promise when he and her sister first married. Told how his daddy was a politician. Not a local politician but one who represented Kentucky. I was told how he liked Teddy Roosevelt. His father had to return because his wife had died delivering their ninth child. That event changed my great-grandpa. According to her, he was never the same. He just stayed around the place and pined himself away. She said the way she had gone haunted him until his neighbor and lifelong friend shot him over a property dispute. They each claimed the other owned the land. Shot him after their disagreement when he returned with a gun. Killed in front of his children, then was acquitted because of self-defense. One fatal shot changed the outcome of nine children, with my grandfather being the fifth of the nine. When he saw his father murdered, he was at the age when a man saw what he wanted to become, and the world noticed that gleam in his eyes. She told from then on, he lived the life of a man with something to prove. Described how the more he did to prove it, the more he fell from grace. She said working in the steel mill was doing the devil's business. She believed, as did her mother, that God intended men to live off their land, and they had no respect for a man who would gamble his life away working in a factory.

Things that woman told me were awful. She said how grandma tried to rescue every stranger. How she'd take them in and believe every detail of their harrowing story. How she'd feed them and give to them even though it meant she would have to neglect her children. All the things she told and never once mentioned why they parted ways. I was told that my grandparents got along before he passed. Still, whenever he returned to the home he purchased for them, my great-grandmother stood in the pathway, threatening to kill him with her hatchet, swearing he better not step foot on her property. I was told how he returned for vacations, begging grandma to come with him in earlier days, but he always returned to the mill alone. She said he came home long enough to make another child and leave for city life. Such things weren't hard for me to grasp; I was used to being raised in a house full of strangers. Still, I often wondered if, at one time, Grandma wasn't my great-uncle's secret love. It is not natural to have such a consuming passion.

I could only imagine Him standing at the fence line of the place he bought, watching her mother tending to her loving pot, talking to her daughter, and teaching her how best to prepare her morsels of knowledge to guide them throughout existence. I could see my great-grandmother's hint of a smile as she developed her torture. I see her studying, watching one of her children slither silently in to drink from her overflowing caldrons. I viewed my great-grandmother laughing as her girl scampered off to face the world they created with the dark knowledge some thought was stolen from the dregs of her loving- pot.

I preferred to go to something other than my grandma's sister's place. I am trying to understand why we did. We sure were not wanted or welcomed. Still, that is the only place I know of where grandma did not act as though she owned the keys to the castle.

Chapter 54

Like many others, I wondered who my grandparents were. I was also unwilling to look into the matter because I might be better off not knowing if they were evil. There are problems with our family's secrecy. Our family uses lies to help stir confusion and create a natural hindrance to progress. When I tried to inquire about a past relative, I was constantly presented with conflicting stories. Though I have never met those relatives, I know enough about the ones telling the stories to realize they have never dared to question the stories they were taught.

Occasionally we would all be loaded in a car to visit an old person or place. Grandma would know some person or knew someone the person once loved or thought they knew. They would begin talking, and I'd be instructed to go busy myself. I just realized the importance of our past in plotting a future. My great aunt has said Grandma was once a wild one. Some of the things grandma's sister said she did were embarrassing to me. We were told how grandma walked about with a lusty smell of pleasure still on her. My great-aunt claimed grandma did not help her man; she completed his destruction. The things she and the others who claimed to love grandma told had me questioning their love.

Grandma was different. I figured she'd called me things that were said about her. We never found the right moment to talk about it, but I knew that mom also was a child of divorced parents. Mom also knew the loneliness of rejection for what others did or did not do. Sometimes, I wish I had learned how to talk with her, but what would a child know concerning life, love, or loss? I was another child being raised in the shadows. What could I possibly know about life? Then again, things came back to kick us whenever we tried to talk.

Grandma was sometimes right. She was the head night cook at the best restaurant/bar in town. Grandma was a big woman. She was not fat. The Queen was big. Stood about six foot four and not a petite inch on her. The man who owned the restraint and she were friends. Apparently, they had some hard times together. I am still determining exactly what their bond was. Still, several members of her family had worked or still worked there at that time. There was a rich guy who would come in but would leave with the salt and pepper shakers and take the silverware for good measure. The owner told the staff he wanted it stopped and explained that he didn't care if the guy returned. While taking her to work the next day, grandma had mom stop at a grocery after explaining that she needed a few things. When she got to the restraint, she told the others if the guy came, she wanted to know. When the guy came into the restaurant, grandma served him. It is said that grandma went out and stripped the table of everything. He had to use plastic utensils to eat with. He received the complementary bread, but it was not in a basket. Not even an extra chair was left at his table. She served the man whatever he ordered and assigned her dishwasher to watch over him. When the guy requested salt and pepper, it had to be returned to his guard immediately after use. When the embarrassed and irate man went to pay his check, grandma was at the cash register. The man complained rather loudly about being served on paper plates with plastic utensils. Grandma is rumored to have explained to the room that as soon as the man returned with all the silverware and salt and pepper shaker he had taken, the restraint would once again offer him the quality of service the other dinners enjoyed at a reasonable price.

On another occasion, a man came in regularly for his T-bone meals. He happened to prefer them rare and demanded they only briefly touch the grill. Whenever his stake came, he would eat the meat around the bone and then return his stake, requesting another because that one had been overcooked and was challenging. The man knew the stake could not be placed back on the grill. He would use the same tactic to get one more and then leave, pretending to be upset. This brought to grandma. The next time she received his standard order, she went to the doorway and entered the dining area. She then prepared his potato and vegetables and grabbed his steak straight from the chiller. She took him his meal, but when the steak was placed on the table, she picked it up with her tongs and passed a match under it once, then demanded to know from the five foot-two one-hundred-twenty-pound man if that stake was rare enough.

That said, I must tell you that grandma fed our garbage men. She could have set out the Empire State building, and they would have taken it. Once when I was younger, they refused to pick up any can that weighed over seventy pounds before becoming Sanitation engineers. At this time, trash had to be in their prescribed containers. I sat out our waste that day, but they said they could not take it because it was too heavy. I told them I understood and that they shouldn't worry because I'd explain it to grandma, and she would bring the trash back to the house and figure out something. Whatever trash grandma sat out was taken because grandma fed the garbage men. Three fried eggs, strips of bacon, sausage, or ham steaks with home-fried potatoes, homemade cathead bisects, and gravy. While the men ate, she filled their thermoses with freshly brewed coffee and knew how each preferred theirs. Whatever grandma sat out was taken. Grandma fed the garbage men and was not concerned with the man who had to traverse the treacherous mountain passes to pick her coffee beans at their peak of perfection. Grandma did not look past the moment. She did not care where it had come from. She did not anticipate where it was heading. Grandma lived in the moment and would let everything else fall wherever it fell.

Chapter 55

Being out in the world forces one to discover the need to learn how to read people. It is easy to hear disgust and laughter in someone's eyes. Seeing the entrapment or danger some smiles hide is not so easy. I was taught young to ignore the faces and watch the body's movement. The delivery of words can tell more than the words could ever express. That being said, there are people I am at peace with. I do not know why, but I am. Then again, some people set me on edge.

I was forced to learn to read people, to absorb how they reacted within their atmosphere. I sought things out of balance. Instability breeds opportunity. Opportunities can indeed be good or bad. I am not saying that I avoided avoiding possibilities. I did so with extreme caution when I approached an out-of-kilter situation. I said this to say a grave danger comes through the written word. This danger comes through the limitation of it having one perspective. Words create a one-dimensional image. Life, however, is multi-dimensional. One should resist the tendency to form conclusions hastily and allow the terms to establish their flow. History books are filled with reasons why we should welcome opposing views. History often is written by those who thought they had won the battles. Yet, many never observe the egos of winners and seldom present others with the freedom to expose all their traits.

Abusers become their own victims. It may take a while, but given time, one realizes they slowly but surely build their own hells. It would be easier to sit back, take all their information in, and cast a judgment. It is easy to look out and see the wrong; a moment's judgment screams needs to be corrected. What is the likelihood that looking out will ever change our world? We need to remove ourselves from the equation. We are easily affected by our pains. It is irrational to allow eternal events to unravel eternal truths. The old saying is, "Those who do not know their history are destined to repeat it." We have to accept our past. We have to realize that the past is not good. It is not evil. It's indifferent. This indifference permits safety while gleaning from its imagery. Information for changing the future needs to be gathered from the past. If the definition of insanity is to repeat an action while expecting different results. It is unwise to strive to move forward without searching the past for direction. It is easier to maintain the cycle than to braze the new course.

Chapter 56

Early in my childhood, I was taught the need to hide. This need to hide for self-preservation was established before I entered the first grade. Some foolish thing would happen. One of us would be hit, and though I cannot recall the delivery, I cannot forget the results. My brother seemed to get punished for something, and mom would go in. I would try to hide and not hear the sounds of the beating. It is normal to stand for your principles, but to demand to be abused so another may receive a moment of relief to gather their thoughts is unreasonable.

Fighting for your principles, I understand. There are moments when we must defend our rights. Moments when truth calls us to stand. When such moments come, we must stand, even if it means we stand alone. To fight to relieve oneself from boredom may or may not be correct. It once served a purpose, even if the objective was to try to feel again. To fight to steal or take what is not rightfully yours leaves one angry. Anger turns to depression and shows a lack of knowledge of how everything comes together to create the whole. I agree some of the wrongs of the past have helped in honing today's image; however, I could not grasp that as a child. Viewing the house's injustice was not self-defeating; it was depressing. I would go walking, and someone would ask what was wrong. Then I'd hear the wrong being excused by clichés.' When I was a kid..." or, "Don't you worry, things will work out." The people asked so they could talk; they did not listen to what I was saying. I believed a certain amount of ignorance came with being a grown-up. Somehow, they had forgotten what it was like to be a kid. They forget how dependent we are despite our appearance. Truth has never been pleasing, but it is easier to swallow than denial. I used to believe that someday, someone would figure it out. They never did or always knew and acted like they didn't.

Chapter 57

When I was in the second grade, a girl wrote a play about a fish struggling to find its family. We were forced to watch it at school. Her script was received well by the teachers and parents. The parents who came to the PTA meeting had to watch it, also. All that time in school and, the fish didn't know what the street taught. That fish swam around and was always missing its parents. Was the thing blind? Could it not see the hooks in the water? Did it grasp that other fish were waiting for their chance to devour it? The audience clapped in approval. People smiled as they passed by her to acknowledge her achievement. Later in the year, she was brought upon the stage to receive her certificate. The thing was beyond me. I knew I could never tell them what I had learned.

For years after the play, teachers would ask her if she had written anything new. She told most of them she hadn't. She couldn't find the time or the serenity writing demands with all the accolades pouring in from her first masterpiece. She was a lovely girl, though one of the tallest in our class. She was skinny and lightly freckled with brown hair with red undertones when the sun hit it just right. Her hair was cut off her shoulders and given an inward flip to better frame her face. Those curls bounced, though her hair did not swing when she walked. I was in the second grade, and the world had already shown me that only some were understood when they spoke. The uselessness of trying to be understood taught me to show only the shallow imagery I did not care about. I'd begun telling them only what they needed to hear, hoping they'd get on with their existence and leave me alone to try and discover the secrets of life.

I watched that girl. In the beginning, she was proud. Her mom came by the school to pick her up in the new cream-colored station wagon with the faux wooden side panels. Picked her up to take her two blocks away. The teachers told her and her mother how proud they were to have a writer in their class. It seemed fun for her at first. By the fourth grade, she was called upon to answer all hard English questions, and teachers insisted that she be given the leading female roles in school plays. Then, she was no longer a kid. Somewhere, somehow, she became the school's child of promise. I could read the despair in her eyes. She no longer spoke as openly. She became lost in the image she helped to create. Lost in a false reality, she refused to destroy.

Junior high was an eye full. To watch our big fish from the little pond discover she was another little fish in the bigger pond. To observe her struggle to obtain an identity that most kids who once knew her had grown uncomfortable with was disarming. School plays became musicals. Teeth began to glisten with the silvery gleam of braces. Our starting playwright needed to catch up with the crowd. She fought to return until she discovered her friends had accepted being abandoned, as she needed to admit she was forgotten. She was a tall, skinny girl whose face was lightly freckled with brown hair and a red undertone when the sun hit it just right, but she could not sing.

Chapter 58

When I went to school, we were not merely graded on achieving the correct answers; we had to arrive at these answers through the approved method of thought. I got in trouble for solving a short division problem when the teacher had only shown us the long division method. I could not fathom why anyone who knew short-division would choose to use long division. The teacher asked why I was so passionate about using short division. I answered something to the effect that the school was preparing me for the real world. Then asked why it would expose me to a system that leaves me more vulnerable to error. She smiled and agreed that I could use short division from then on. That said, when I went to school, I had to choose my battles and smokescreens. The truth was dad taught me division earlier, and I simply refused to allow them to take away a gift Dad had given.

Chapter 59

In kindergarten, we played with anyone who entered our sandbox. By the sixth grade, our school's system societies had been formed. The schools claimed to teach reading, writing, and arithmetic, then they claimed to add music, art, and history. They introduced a lot more. They taught class structure, hypocrisy, and the danger of thinking outside their box. They introduced this with the aide from their sacred contagion. Once a year, we were taught about the man who could not tell a lie and how he cut down his father's cherry tree. A few years later, we discovered that people used that story as a political ploy. After this, our teachers tried to convince us we should trust them.

I studied a little about Mr. Washington. Many would claim George lives a charmed life. I still preferred our third president over him. He gave more to our country than Washington did. I will concede that Washington was our first president. It is shown that he served two successful terms. Then again, the war was not fought to create a new kingdom. It was opposed to granting us liberty. When Washington's terms were up, he went home. Our third president served under the first two before being elected himself. It was his pinned words that dared to define the terms of our revolution. I do have trouble with a few losses he endured because of the struggles he had within himself. I also have found a few contradictions within myself.

Chapter 60

I can recall the pain expressed by faceless strangers as they came to school mid-year. This became harder after the third grade when our society had been formed. Third grade was where teachers entered into the separation of the inter cultures. A new kid did not stand a chance of replacing an old standby on our school's teams. Once, two brothers moved into a two-story about five blocks from us. They came from out of state. The younger brother was my age. Their dad worked for the phone company and could get us things. His truck had this rubber tubing stuff far superior to old cut bike enter tubes for making slingshots. Their dad would cut the bodies for our weapons out of plywood. Between us, we put together some great slingshots. We discovered the need for a ball bearing tied in the tube to give it extra strength to withstand our pulls.

We used to line up cans and bottles for targets until we discovered the implosion of shooting out a TV's picture tube. Witnessing what a marble could cause was beyond what we could imagine.

I continued to hang out with these two until I heard about some kids who had lost their cat. It was a tabby cat. I listened to the story of how the oldest brother killed it. I never inquired whether it was accidental or on purpose. The fact is, I never even asked if he did it. The cat was the pet of three kids who lived in a little white house beside the alley about half a block from their home. Those kids repeatedly asked everyone about their cat. I do not know if he did it, but he was mean enough. I haven't made or shot a slingshot since.

Chapter 61

While in school and under the fifth grade, yet a
full-day student, we had music lessons on Tuesdays
and Thursdays. In fifth and sixth grade, these classes
became Band or orchestra. Our music teacher was an
older lady with fiery orange hair that had little silver
glimmering streaks created by those few that escaped
the coloring. She was a short-rounded woman with
glasses swinging from a chain. The only other thing
she could have done to warn us as to who she was
would have been to own a pair of those horned-rim
glasses and park her broom in the corner. She would
walk about our classroom holding an opened piece of
music while singing loudly. She glared at us students
over the sheet music as she tried to prance about in
time with the music. I can't recall her ever once
putting on her glasses. I was also amazed that
someone with a voice like that was able to hear
someone else off-key.

On Mondays and Fridays, we had art. She was a
young teacher who looked more like a high school
student than a teacher. She could drawl. She brought
freedom and freshness back into our lives. We could
draw, paint, color, or sculpt something out of
modeling clay. Even though she would help us
accomplish a task, she was no pushover. She taught
me the importance of viewing things in their proper
perspective. She taught us how to drawl by reducing
things to the basic outlines of their shapes. She proved
to me the importance of sketching an image lightly

then returning to establish the lines. Her husband was killed. He was shot down. The school told her she was not to talk about it with us. They claimed we were too young to understand. We tried to help her, but we were a bunch of kids. The music teacher came to class the next day with some nice writing paper. She told us that our class would be different that day because we were to write a note to our art teacher, fold it once, and put it in the box on the teacher's desk. She then started telling us what not to do with the paper. By the time she finished with her instructions, half of the class period was over, and she had turned a good thing into an ordeal I was not sure I wanted any part of. I told the teacher some of the things I'd seen but confided that I didn't have a clue about what she was going through. I told her I really didn't know what to say. Then I thanked her because I knew she would understand because she was the type of person who makes our world a little better place. It may be because of her that I like the feeling of free art. I have been told such is an acquired taste. Personally, I believe some things are known, and others must come to you. I don't accept that everything is taught. Somethings just come to us. If this is not so then there could be no advancement of mankind.

Chapter 62

I also remember an old man who had snow-white hair and would sit out on his porch. He had one of those gliders, but he simply sat in his. He would be out there come evening to feel the cool air and let its breeze carry his cares away. Beside his glider was a small round table. On I would be a tall glass of tea with ice and a slice of lemon stuck on its rim. Somewhere near by the tea he seemed to be compelled to have a small plate of cookies. The old man never wore a hat, and his glasses were usually off and sitting on the little table, upside-down. When I'd walk by, he'd tilt his head just enough to form a nod.

I liked the old man. His face was carved by life. He hadn't a whisker to be seen, but his face was one in a million. He had the look which would have made a photographer well-known. I do not recall ever actually speaking to him, but we had a silent understanding. His house was well-kept and had a huge window in the center of what I always imagined to be his living room. This baby grand piano was centered on the window. I pictured him as the man who lived in glass because the world on the other side of that window did not concern his view. The papers were reporting how many had died overseas. People were rioting in the big cities. Kids were shot at the college up the road as he quietly sat in his glider. He wore nice dress shoes but did not keep them perfectly shined. His slacks were of the dress style, and he wore a nice shirt without the tie. The man never appeared to be wrung out. I don't recall him ever reading anything while he sat. He just sat, sipping his tea while periodically taking a nibble from a cookie. I often questioned if he was as fascinated by those he watched as I was by him. He was a quiet man unless you considered his face and the history it told. I liked the man, though I was careful around him. He seemed to understand more than people wanted to be told. I would have loved to have been invited up to his glider and listen to the things his years of living had caused him to suspect. Something about the old boy captured my interest. To me, he was more than an old man who sat motionless on his glider, nibbling cookies and drinking tea. To me, he was a friend. Though we never spoke, except through our quick nods. Still, I liked the old man who lived in glass.

Chapter 63

As a kid, I had a summer when I was planning to run away. It was the summer between the fifth and sixth grades. I planned on holding up in a small, wooded area near where I used to escape to go fishing. In school, we had to read a book about a guy who held up in the hollow of a tree. Another kid and I were going to escape our existences and return to society when we were men of eighteen or so. He and I divided the tasks needed to be accomplished to live independently. We went to the library to do research. I went to the creek, and a tree across the stream fell below our fishing hole to help create what might be loosely called a dam. I also took an old Army shovel and began a trickle where water would run over some rocks to help purify it. That task was abandoned when I discovered the creeks' water source bubbling up amongst some sedimentary rocks near a small cliff a little upstream. I chose the perfect spot to begin the work of building our shelter. It was protected from the wind and had two natural ways of escape. I planned on leaving everything behind and returning when I had something to say. However, during research, I was struck by a crazy question, "How much freedom would be gained by living as though others did not exist? Running away ceased being an option. I had figured, to my own satisfaction, how to survive. The answer caused me to be more aware of our interdependence. There is a type of freedom that demands that we become slaves to existence, which might be why our forefathers fought for liberty.

Chapter 64

The child's advocate asked that I give her an informed opinion of a person's action I knew thirty-five years prior. She asked for this without explaining what my cousin, once removed, was being accused of. I found it strange how she preferred opinion over recent facts. I sensed that I had insulted her by giving her the assignment to look up events in our family's history. She took the information quite differently than the lady from the FBI. She complained that the state's recorded information needed to be made available. She said the period was before it would have been recorded on computers. I wonder if she presumed, I believed it was before thought or a filing system. I was informed of the mounds of paperwork. I was reminded of the system's insufficiency in doing what people believed they did. I was surprised that she had not researched the old newspapers to get important dates and facts to fill in the details she claimed she needed more.

She wanted to know if I thought he could commit such undefined crimes. I told her what I once knew would not prove her case beyond a reasonable doubt. She said she wanted background information. I assumed she had already read his profile and was trying to add color and depth to her image. She informed me that she thought a slight dysfunction ran through our family members. I dread that politically correct language; it can make a molehill out of a mountain. She then explained that my personal history was insignificant and wanted my opinion. I told her to contact a significant person and to lose my name and number. Her system did not work for me in the past, and I held no delusion it would be up and running to help any victim anytime soon.

If all the abused in our communities were gathered and asked to write a short paper on who was the source of their most significant pain, I venture to say many would be surprised at how poorly our system is conceived by those it claims to help. Our approach is portrayed to consist of overworked, understaffed employees striving to solve our society's problems while being forced to stay within guidelines of a concept that some distant ones want to be heroes suffering from delusions of grandeur created. Slice the image however you wish; it does not spell reform. Given the odds, the average abused child in our system would not bet that our system could pour water out of a boot if given a memo stating the instructions were typed in triplicate and attached to the heel.

Their employees apologize for the system. It is usually not good when a government employee starts their sentence with, "I'm sorry, but...." The irony is I've never met one of the systems that knew its workings and claimed it functioned properly. Everyone who knew the system agreed. The design remains inept because the system is viewed as incompetent and used by people doing their own thing and trying to change the system from within. The truth remains that the system is part of the problem, not the solution. It is easily manipulated. There were times when I could hear the Queen plotting. They would sit around our table, drinking coffee and eating food we were not allowed to have, working out their parts in the following scheme. Sometimes, they came together to get something from the other for themselves. Mostly, they schemed for the mere pleasure of humiliating one another. There were no permanent teams. Sides were chosen as the situations demanded. There was no loyalty, only the necessity to cover each other from an outsider's view. They were ruled by desires and searched for victims to welcome to their webs. They would do little things to let the prey feel at ease, become comfortable, and forget where they were. I could hear their voices whispering soft words amazed me at how they would surprise their prey. Today, some forty-odd years later, if Grandma or one of the queens enters my dream, it jolts me awake, and I must calm myself to get back to sleep.

The queens gathered like some tribal ritual to torment the captured, believing the strength of the excited victim was in their blood. The hunt never appeared to be about them. They never would portray themselves as the ones in need. They were viewed as acting out of concern for others and wanted to know if we were willing to do without so they could be portrayed as making a generous contribution. Not once could they be questioned. Not once was it permitted that we who sacrificed be allowed to deliver our assistance. Such would have exposed the Queen, and her judgment was not to be questioned. After the trap was sprung, they would gather to replay their parts and divide the spoils. There were moments when the spoil was merely another's self-esteem, but it laid the foundation for their next quest. I have seen them inviting someone into their group to humiliate them for wanting to belong. I have seen many crumbling at their table while wondering if they would ever amount to anything. I have witnessed the silent, trembling lips holding back screams and fear through downcast eyes. Theirs is a sadistic game. It is played by people who think they are made more prominent by belittling another. People who never realize they are amongst the captured.

We are all connected. We all come together to create the whole. Without the horror, I do not know that I would have sought to change my views. My uncle warned, life without death becomes absurd." If not for the pain of death, I might not have known to strive for life.

Chapter 65

We had a faceless clock in our living room, which chimed to announce the passing of another quarter hour. Its face was ornate. It had a beautifully carved case from amongst the most skillful Bavarian craftsmen. A pendulum swung back and forth, marching behind the leaded glass each second. It had etched in Roman numerals filled with gold. The key for winding it was kept on a little shelf, which the front door blocked from view until it was opened. Seven turns of the key on each of the three pins kept the clock in time for eight days, providing no one re-adjusted the pendulum.

I remember lying in bed listening to the sounds of that clock. It would aimlessly tick away the seconds. Before its chimes sang, there would be a hush and then the whirling, varying lengths depending on the times the chimes would sing. Carved birds sat silently in their faceless carved-out forest. They looked and guarded the onlookers of their faceless world. Most such clocks had faces and opened eyes and puffy cheeks attempting to blow back the clouds of time, but not ours. The look on our clock was the view of some distant mountains to be climbed. Its rich dark brown wood promised life beyond living as its pendulum marched in a new second. Our clock did not need eyes. The birds in the forest told the story. Eyes in the house were useless because our lips had never parted with the secrets of what had been branded upon our brains. The birds in the branches did not become alarmed by the passing of time. The swaying of the pendulum did not disturb the birds as we silently awaited the moment we would be freed.

Beside the clock was a painting. An old man sat at his table with his hands folded, head bowed, and eyes closed. His glasses were on his closed bible, but his lips never formed to say a word. The old man just hung beside the clock, unaffected by the passage of time. A piano stayed in the corner, with stories to tell and memories to lift, but no one in the house played that piano. Besides the piano was Grandma's chair, and behind the chair were the stairs or the way of escape. You had to get past Grandma to do anything in the house, including leaving. We had a big yard but couldn't play in it. If we got out, we were gone. My brother hid in the attic room if he was home. Sometimes, his friends came over, but the house figured his friends caused his demise, so that door was closed to the rest of us. I knew the time by knowing the trains. At night, you could hear the trains announcing they were coming to town. The nine fifteen reported our time to return. The twelve-five was our train of rest. After the twelve-five went through the house, slept, and it was safe again until morning. I would listen to the hounds and crickets at night, but when I heard the car door, I tried to close my ears. Shut my eyes and remind my brain it was time to shut down. When I watched shows, when someone faced death, they seemed to see their life pass before them. It did not happen like that to me. A few times, I accepted that I was going to die. I did not fight back; I received it. There was no fear, flashbacks, or longing for another breath, just a calm acceptance of death. It was almost as though I was welcoming it. At night we used to lie awake listening for the twelve-five. Before it came through, Grandma would return from work with the meatiest stake bone for the dog. He lived to ride to go get grandma from work, but we just lay in bed listening for the train. After the trees had lost their leaves in the fall, I used to peer out the window at those who walked our street at night. Their heads would be tucked into the collars of their coats, and their shoulder would be up as though they could protect their heads from the cold. It was hard to walk our streets at night and not feel the world's evil closing in with each overhanging branch of the trees reaching out to snatch life from the unaware. Their limbs became branches, and those branches grew into fingers. The sounds of cur, hounds, of owls in the trees all sounded different in the shadows of those overhanging lifeless trees. Even the glow of streetlights shone eerie in the fall. The glowing crept from pole to pole, reminding us of things that happened to others under a full moon. People often would pull their coat collars up and blind themselves of their peripheral view to avoid being reminded of where they were. They did not really walk; it was more of a trot from wherever they had been to wherever they were going. They all seemed to come to the same conclusion under the trees: People need not meander on streets alone at night. You could hear the sounds of cars in the distance, and sirens announced that all was not well. All the while, the faceless clock of our living room kept in time with the world inside its walls.

Chapter 66

The trucker came to our part of town and parked his rig in front of the wooded area we called the fort. He climbed out and walked down the street as though nothing had better confront him. He stayed away about three hours, and when he returned, he had his arm around some hunkering woman. She was wearing a sailor's coat, and her rusty color skirt barely peeked out from under it. They climbed into the cab using the same door. She must have gone straight for the sleeper. He warmed the truck and then pulled away. I never saw her face, but her bleached blond hair could be seen on the collar of her navy coat. About four days later, they discovered a bleach-blond lady leaning against a telephone pole outside town. The paper only showed an artist's rendering of her body. I did not trust the man who climbed out of the truck, but I had not seen the lady close enough to know if it was her. The paper would print a description of the victims then the town would bury them in the far back corner of the graveyard.

Our old graveyard had a rod iron fence around it, and the tombstones told more than the markers in the new cemetery. My brother's body is in the new one. Beside the old graveyard is railroad tracks. Next to them is a candy store. Across the street from it is a gas station. When you pulled in to get gas, a slender man hobbled over to clean your windshield while inquiring what else he might do for you. While the gas was pumping, he'd check your oil, then the other fluids, and kick the tires. He moved differently because he left part of his leg in Korea, and the one he was given to replace it didn't bend.

His face was distorted on the left side from a car wreck that took his wife's life. When he was finished gassing up your car and had given it the once over, he would hand the driver some green stamps, which were suitable for valuable merchandise, we were told, but my mean aunt kept stealing ours so she could get the things she told grandma she needed. They said the man at the gas station did not have much of a life. Said he slept in the back room behind the service bays. He couldn't do much work in the service bays, so he hobbled about doing what he could and talking with those who came in to get gas. He knew when a more pronounced limp would be needed to secure a larger tip. He knew whose car or truck was for sale and the cost. He knew the excellent deals and the deals to stay away from. More car deals were made at his pumps than at the used car lots outside town. He would be out pumping when another new car owner would stop by to thank him for all his help. After shaking their hand, he always put his hand back into his right-hand pants pocket. People said he was a quiet man. They felt obligated to have him try to sell their old cars after he found them such a sweet deal on their new ones. He only spoke concerning his business, which others may have confused with pumping gas. The quiet man amassed a tidy sum. He never retired. He moved into one of his beachfront beach properties down in FT Lauderdale.

At this time, the world outside the house grew large, and the house itself shrunk. There were places to be and things yearning to be explored. I had places to go where the house had never been. It was becoming a big, expanding world beyond the attic room's view. I was being called to go.

I discovered it, at times, is best to get out of the way of someone's slide and leave things alone to allow human nature to take its course. I was fishing at the river when my cousin's husband came upon me and decided to bother me. I minded my own business when this man twice my age started in. I tried to simply walk away, but he followed. He told me he was going to get me on my way home. There weren't any cell phones, no 911 calls. However, some of the regulars at the river knew me, but not the stranger. As they happened to walk by, they would inquire if things were all right. I told them everything was fine, but he had forgotten his medicines, and I had to wait until someone came and helped him. I told them everything was OK and that we could generally speak because he was almost deaf and needed to be closer to read our lips. He was too far off to make out what we were saying. The fact that he was watching me let me know something was happening at the house. I slowly walked him to the golf course by walking downstream. I continued walking, pretending to fish in spots until I had him near the golf course's clubhouse. People would slowly walk by him and yell hello while overemphasizing their facial expressions. Someone came and asked what was wrong. I told them I did not know but was surprised they let him out this long without his medications. It was not long until the actions of strangers had him in a foul mood. He glared at people who thought they were helping. The firemen came with the police. Rumors were someone at the golf course claimed he was scaring their children. Rumors started flying. The river people disappeared as human nature began to take its course. Someone tried to ascertain if he needed any medical attention. He yelled back the wrong answer, or at least it was one with a bad attitude. People had been going to complain about him to the staff, and when he got clever with the cop, the party ended. It was determined that he needed a vacation from the world, and he was given a few days' stay at the county's hospital's mental ward. When I got to the house, I discovered a deal had been made. We were going to help them purchase a lovely new brick house. Their neighborhood was unsafe to bring a child up in, even though he was being raised at home. That boy was a gold mine. They dangled that kid and threatened to take him away and obtain whatever they wanted. He was a kid and did not understand his part in their arrangements. The only time he knew something was up was when he had to go with them for a weekend; that did not happen often, and the first time came after he was three.

Do the others know where her husband went that weekend? When I asked, she said he was helping one of his friends move. I never let on that I knew. Some of the best tricks played on people are by those who never feel the need to take a bow. Besides, they needed to find out who did him in. They blamed someone at the clubhouse, and I had no reason to expose the setup. I am sure he never viewed his part. It is far easier to blame others for his error. Still, we can only change ourselves and hope the difference will inspire others to follow. The next time they came over, he was a little more sheepish than usual as he followed his wife like a lost puppy. He never picked up his head the entire time they were there, and he did not bother to try to go in to sit at the table. He just stayed in the garage and talked to Mom. He had to speak to me occasionally to protect his image. I listened to the nothingness of his words while those at the table agreed upon the final terms to be broken.

Chapter 67

Mom finally came into the house after hearing one of her boys died, so she tried to gather herself and determine which of us was dead. Once she knew, she looked towards the ceiling and asked God why He had taken the only one she ever loved. I could not help but question if it would have been easier if it had been me. I watched the people coming over, knowing I was being protected by the gathering. Those at the table gathered to make plans for my brother's services. They stated it would be a private service for family members only. They made all the decisions. Mom paid all the bills, yet only two at the table lived in the house, and Grandma was not a family member.

I began being forceful in voicing my opinions. Their planning subsided. The following day, before the table had gathered, my oldest sister had gone to the doctor and had gotten him to give her something for me to take the edge off. They achieved their goal, but they took everything else off with that edge. Days are missing from memory, and most of the following week is gone. I don't recall having an advantage. I recall being upset about others outside of our family making choices, and my opinion was not allowed to be uttered. I remember going after the cop who announced death from the curb. I remember begging them to let me go and identify my brother's body and them allowing a queen to go. They told me I was too young and could not do it. I never thought it was right to not permit his friends to come to the services; not even his girlfriend was allowed to say goodbye. It appeared to me the house was punishing the ones who knew and loved him for his death. I thought it was disrespectful that the only ones permitted to come were dad's and mom's family members, who were, for the most part, strangers to us' and or the extended family member who had kicked us our entire lives. Mom told our preacher we wanted a salvation message, but I am not sure the sermon was heard over the silent screams from the house. It was odd, the things people will tell a kid. I was told God had a good reason for taking him by someone I didn't know knew God existed. I was told that it was for the best that he died because we did not know what his life would have become by someone who did not appear to be attempting suicide.

COMING SOON:

MY NAME IS JACKSON

The Cost of Escape

ACKNOWLEDGEMENTS

Andreas Kossak for his calming support, constant encouragement to write it again, and teaching techniques to make it clearer. (A Writers Guild of America member, Andreas is the author of screenplays and fiction.)

John Cole for the boot in the ass. (John is the author of the six-novel series *A Teller's Tales* and a book of poetry, *Giants and Friends*.)

Suzy Pearce and **Jeff McCarley** for their unending moral support. (Suzy is the author of the novels *Air* and *Toxic*, the short story collection *This is Not the End,* and the co-author with Jeff McCarley of the screenplay *Rose*. Jeff is the author of *People Suck*, *I am Disgusting*, and the novel *The Hearty Bros*.)

Pete Schreiber for being a gentleman. He was such an encouragement when the Written By Veterans group heard about this project. (Pete is the author of the forthcoming biographical screenplay *The Crossroads,* set during the WWII Battle of the Bulge.)

Cindy Rinne for being a beautiful person who understands that we are to help one another when we can, not only when it is easy. (Cindy is the author of numerous poetry books. She was Poet in Residence for the Neutra Institute Gallery and Museum, Los Angeles, and is a nominee for a Pushcart award.)

John J. McBrearty (COL Mack) for being a man with so many irons in the fire but still being willing to stop and lift a fellow soldier. (COL Mack is the author of several book series, including the American History, A Veterans Perspective series, the four-volume Combat Journal, and a series on Children's Golf. I would like to reference all his published books, but their number is constantly growing.)

Fred Dunning, for his encouraging words, understanding, and ability to look me in the eyes and say, "By writing this story, you are doing a good thing. You'll never know how rare it is that someone survived these things and will talk about them." I find that I will write about them, but I don't really like to talk about them. I have to stop my conversation at times because, even after these many years have passed, my emotions still run deep. (Mr. Dunning, Bo, as he is known to me, is the author of seven books on Veteran issues ranging from married life and PTSD to navigating the Veterans Administration red tape road, as well as the popular *51 Stupid Questions People Ask Veterans*.)

Al Rattan, because he listens and gives encouraging words that make sense. And because, of all things, he is a retired Policeman. We may approach trouble from different perspectives, but he and I agree on many points on how to correct it. (Al is the author of the biographical novel *Mitchell Porter,* set during the American Revolution)

ABOUT THE AUTHOR

Born in Troy, Ohio, J. L. Erwin served in the U. S. Army as a member of a special weapons team and was part of a supporting unit for NATO.

J. L. Erwin earned his BA and MBA degrees from California State University, San Bernardino. He is a lifetime member of Beta Gamma Sigma since 2020 and has served as the Student Veterans Organization's president.

Other Books by J.L. Erwin

Still – Poetry and Prose

"*J. L Erwin writes tender prose and poems about his first love whose life was cut short before the full bloom of their relationship. He relishes her as she brought beauty into his world without judgement. They met several years ago, but Joe still lights up when sharing about her. In this book, his sensitive and beautiful words give breath to death. "The grave will never understand / love doesn't yield to its defeating."*
--CINDY RINNE, Author of *The Feather Ladder*

Available on Amazon

Made in the USA
Columbia, SC
15 March 2024

33095169R00224